THE SKILLS OF DIAGNOSTIC PLANNING

THE SKILLS OF DIAGNOSTIC PLANNING

PSYCHIATRIC REHABILITATION PRACTICE SERIES:book 1

William A. Anthony, Ph.D.
Director, Center for Rehabilitation Research and
   Training in Mental Health
Associate Professor
Department of Rehabilitation Counseling
Sargent College of Allied Health Professions
Boston University

Richard M. Pierce, Ph.D.
Director of Training Services
Carkhuff Institute of Human Technology
Amherst, Massachusetts

Mikal R. Cohen, Ph.D.
Director of Training, Center for Rehabilitation Research
   and Training in Mental Health
Research Associate Professor
Department of Rehabilitation Counseling
Sargent College of Allied Health Professions
Boston University

John R. Cannon, Ph.D.
Director of Evaluation
Carkhuff Institute of Human Technology
Amherst, Massachusetts

University Park Press
Baltimore

UNIVERSITY PARK PRESS
International Publishers in Science, Medicine, and Education
233 East Redwood Street
Baltimore, Maryland 21202

This book was developed by the Carkhuff Institute of Human Technology, 22 Amherst Road, Amherst, MA 01002, pursuant to Public Health Service Grant No. T21 MH 14502-20 with the National Institute of Mental Health; Alcohol, Drug Abuse, and Mental Health Administration, Department of Health, Education and Welfare.

THE PSYCHIATRIC REHABILITATION PRACTICE SERIES

Instructor's Guide
by *William A. Anthony, Ph.D.,*
Mikal R. Cohen, Ph.D., and Richard M. Pierce, Ph.D.

Book 1: **The Skills of Diagnostic Planning** / *William A. Anthony, Richard M. Pierce, Mikal R. Cohen, and John R. Cannon*
Book 2: **The Skills of Rehabilitation Programming** / *William A. Anthony, Richard M. Pierce, Mikal R. Cohen, and John R. Cannon*
Book 3: **The Skills of Professional Evaluation** / *Mikal R. Cohen, William A. Anthony, Richard M. Pierce, Leroy A. Spaniol, and John R. Cannon*
Book 4: **The Skills of Career Counseling** / *Richard M. Pierce, Mikal R. Cohen, William A. Anthony, Barry F. Cohen, and Theodore W. Friel*
Book 5: **The Skills of Career Placement** / *Richard M. Pierce, Mikal R. Cohen, William A. Anthony, Barry F. Cohen, and Theodore W. Friel*
Book 6: **The Skills of Community Service Coordination** / *Mikal R. Cohen, Raphael L. Vitalo, William A. Anthony, and Richard M. Pierce*

Library of Congress Cataloging in Publication Data

Anthony, William Alan, 1942–
    The skills of diagnostic planning.
    (Psychiatric rehabilitation practice series; book 1)
    Bibliography: p.
    Includes index.
    1. Mentally ill—Rehabilitation. 2. Personality
assessment. I. Pierce, Richard M., joint author.
II. Cohen, Mikal R., joint author. III. Title.
IV. Series.
[RC439.5.A58]   362.2'04256   79-29692
ISBN 0-8391-1574-1

THE SKILLS OF DIAGNOSTIC PLANNING

CONTENTS

ABOUT THE AUTHORS

Dr. William A. Anthony is an Associate Professor and Director of Clinical Training in the Department of Rehabilitation Counseling, Sargent College of Allied Health Professions, Boston University. Dr. Anthony has been Project Director of a National Institute of Mental Health grant designed to develop and evaluate training materials for persons studying and practicing in the field of Psychiatric Rehabilitation. Dr. Anthony has been involved in the field of Psychiatric Rehabilitation in several different capacities. He has researched various aspects of psychiatric rehabilitation practice and has authored over three dozen articles about psychiatric rehabilitation which have appeared in professional journals.

Dr. Richard M. Pierce is Director of Training Services at the Carkhuff Institute of Human Technology, a non-profit organization dedicated to increasing human effectiveness. Dr. Pierce has extensive counseling experience and has consulted to dozens of local, state and federal human service programs. He has taught the skills and knowledge of psychiatric rehabilitation to practitioners from a variety of disciplines. Dr. Pierce is noted for his research on the training of counselors. Dr. Pierce has authored eight books and dozens of articles in professional journals.

Dr. Mikal R. Cohen is the Director of Rehabilitation and Mental Health Services at the Carkhuff Institute of Human Technology, a non-profit organization dedicated to increasing human effectiveness. Dr. Cohen has been a practitioner in several outpatient and inpatient mental health settings, and has served as an administrator, inservice trainer, program evaluator and consultant to numerous rehabilitation and mental health programs. She has developed teaching curricula and taught the skills of psychiatric rehabilitation to practitioners throughout the United States. Furthermore, Dr. Cohen has authored a number of books and articles in the fields of mental health and health care.

Dr. John R. Cannon is Director of Evaluation at the Carkhuff Institute of Human Technology. Dr. Cannon has extensive experience in both psychology and mental health and has consulted to dozens of local, state and federal human service programs. He has delivered training programs on the skills and knowledge of psychiatric rehabilitation to practitioners from a variety of disciplines. Dr. Cannon is particularly noted for his evaluation studies of human service programs. He has authored ten books and over two dozen articles published in professional journals.

CARKHUFF INSTITUTE of HUMAN TECHNOLOGY

The Carkhuff Institute of Human Technology is intended to serve as a non-profit international center for the creation, development and application of human technology. The Institute, the first of its kind anywhere in the world, takes its impetus from the comprehensive human resource development models of Dr. Robert R. Carkhuff. Using these models as functional prototypes, the Institute's people synthesize human experience and objective technology in the form of a wide range of specific programs and applications.

We live in a complex technological society. Only recently have we begun to recognize and struggle with two crucially important facts: improperly used, our technology creates as many problems as it solves; and this same technology has been delivered to us with no apparent control or "off" buttons. Our attempts to retreat to some pretechnological, purely humanistic state have been both foolish and ill-fated. If we are to develop our resources and actualize our real potential, we must learn to grow in ways which integrate our scientific and applied knowledge about the human condition with the enduring human values which alone can make our growth meaningful.

We cannot afford to waste more time in fragmentary and ill-conceived endeavors. The next several decades — and perhaps far less than that — will be a critical period in our collective history. Recognizing this, the Carkhuff Institute of Human Technology is dedicated to fostering the growth and development of personnel who can develop, plan, implement and evaluate human resource development programs while making direct contributions to the scientific and technological bases of these same programs. Thus the Institute's fundamental mission is to integrate full technical potency with fully human and humane goals — in other words, to deliver skills to people which let them become effective movers and creators rather than impotent victims.

CARKHUFF of INSTITUTE HUMAN TECHNOLOGY

22 AMHERST ROAD
AMHERST, MA 01002
(413) 256-0169

PSYCHIATRIC REHABILITATION PRACTICE SERIES

PREFACE

This text is one of a series of six books designed to facilitate the teaching of various psychiatric rehabilitation skills. It is written for professionals practicing in the field as well as for students studying in such professions as nursing, rehabilitation counseling, occupational therapy, psychology, psychiatry, and social work. Each of these disciplines has contributed and will continue to contribute practitioners, researchers, administrators, and teachers to the field of psychiatric rehabilitation.

This series of training manuals evolved from a lengthy analysis of the practitioner skills that seemed to facilitate the rehabilitation outcome of persons with psychiatric disabilities. Under the sponsorship of the National Institute of Mental Health, each of these training manuals was developed and then field-tested on a group of rehabilitation mental health professionals and students. Based on the feedback of the training participants after the use of these skills with psychiatrically disabled clients, each training manual was revised. Thus, the content of the books reflects not only the authors' perspectives, but also the ideas of the initial group of training participants.

The ultimate purpose of this six-volume series is to improve the rehabilitation services that are presently offered to the psychiatrically disabled person. This training text is written for those practitioners whose rehabilitation mission is either: (1) to assist in the reintegration of the psychiatrically disabled client into the community; or (2) to maintain the ability of the formerly disabled client to continue functioning in the community and, in so doing, to prevent a reoccurrence of psychiatric disability. In other words, depending upon a client's particular situation, psychiatric rehabilitation practitioners attempt either to reduce their clients' dependence on the mental health system or maintain whatever level of independence the clients have already been able to achieve.

This mission can be accomplished when the focus of the psychiatric rehabilitation practitioner's concern is increasing the *skills* and *abilities* of the psychiatrically disabled client. More specifically, the rehabilitation practitioner works to promote the client's ability to employ those skills necessary to live, learn, and/or work in the community. Success is

i

achieved when the client is able to function in the community as independently as possible.

Historically, the primary focus in psychiatric rehabilitation has been on the development of alternative living, learning, and working environments. In such environments, psychiatrically disabled clients have been provided settings in which they can function at a reduced level of skilled performance that is still higher than the level of functioning typically demanded in an institutional setting. In addition, these rehabilitation settings have provided a more humane, active, and "normal" environment within which clients can function. The hope has been that, over a period of time, the more positive environment of these rehabilitation settings might help many clients to improve their ability to function more independently and, in many cases, to actually leave the rehabilitation setting.

Within the last decade, however, rehabilitation has come to involve much more than the development, administration, and coordination of specific settings. Psychiatric rehabilitation practitioners can now assume a direct rehabilitation role by *diagnosing critical skill deficits* in their clients and *prescribing rehabilitation programs* designed to overcome these skill deficits. The development of rehabilitation settings that emphasize the skills and abilities of the clients has helped lay the foundation for this approach to psychiatric rehabilitation.

Although the greatest boon to rehabilitation within the mental health system has been the development of new and unique environmental settings as alternatives to institutional living, the most significant failure of psychiatric rehabilitation has been its inability to train the psychiatric rehabilitation practitioner thoroughly in rehabilitation skills. Professionals from a wide range of disciplines (e.g., counseling, nursing, psychiatry, social work, and psychology) engage in the practice of psychiatric rehabilitation. For the most part, however, these various disciplines have only the expertise developed in their own professions to bring to the field of psychiatric rehabilitation. Their training has lacked a specific set of rehabilitation skills to complement the expertise of their own disciplines.

The present series of psychiatric rehabilitation training texts, of which this volume is a part, is designed to help overcome the lack of specialized training in psychiatric rehabilitation. These training books focus on the specific skills areas that are designed to equip the psychiatric rehabilitation practitioner with the expertise necessary to promote the abilities of the psychiatrically disabled client, either by increasing the client's skills and by modifying the environment so as to better accommodate the client's present level of skilled behavior.

The first two training books help the psychiatric rehabilitation practitioner to become more proficient in *diagnosing* and *teaching* the skills that the client needs to function more effectively in the community. The third book provides the practitioner with the skills necessary to *evaluate* the outcome of her or his rehabilitative efforts. Training books four and five focus specifically on practitioner skills that have been the traditional concern of the rehabilitation practitioner — *career counseling* and *career placement* skills. The sixth training book focuses on ways in which the rehabilitation practitioner can *use the resources of the community* to better accommodate the client's present abilities and programming needs.

Although each text is part of a series of training books, each has been designed so that it may be used independently of the other. The six books included in the series are:

1. **The Skills of Diagnostic Planning**
2. **The Skills of Rehabilitation Programming**
3. **The Skills of Professional Evaluation**
4. **The Skills of Career Counseling**
5. **The Skills of Career Placement**
6. **The Skills of Community Service Coordination**

The skills-learning *process* within the training books involves an explain-demonstrate-practice format. That is, the practitioner is first explained the skill, is then shown examples of the skill, and finally is provided with suggestions on how to practice or do the skill. The practice suggestions include first practicing in a simulated situation and then actually performing the skill with a psychiatrically disabled client.

The first chapter of each training book overviews the specific practitioner skills that comprise that text. The next several chapters of each text are the teaching chapters and present the explain-demonstrate-practice steps involved in learning each specific skill. The final chapter of each book suggests ways in which the practitioner can evaluate one's own or another person's performance of these skills. The reference section of the books contains the major references that are sources of further discussion of various aspects of the skills.

Each of the major teaching chapters has a vignette at the beginning and end of the chapter. This vignette or short story is designed to illustrate unsuccessful and successful applications of the specific skills that are the focus of that particular chapter. Its purpose is to give the reader an overview of the skills that are presented in each chapter. In addition, a summary of the skill behaviors that comprise each major skill is given at the end of each chapter section.

Each chapter contains practice suggestions for each skill that can facilitate the learners' practice of their newly developing skills. Often the learner is first asked to practice and demonstrate her or his skill learning by filling out some type of table or chart. These charts can serve as an observable demonstration of the learner's mastery of a particular skill. Most of these various charts are not needed in the day-to-day application of these skills with actual clients. However, during the skill-learning process, these charts or tables are useful in demonstrating the learner's present level of skill mastery, either to the learner her or himself or to the learner's supervisors and teachers.

The skill-learning *outcome* of each of these training volumes is an observable, measurable cluster of practitioner skills. These skills are not meant to replace the skills of the various disciplines currently involved in the practice of psychiatric rehabilitation; rather, these skills are seen as complementary to the professional's existing skills. The additional use of these rehabilitation skills can play an extremely important role in improving the efficacy of psychiatric rehabilitation.

The Psychiatric Rehabilitation Practice Series has developed out of the contributions of a number of different people. We are particularly indebted to a great many students and practicing professionals, who, by virtue of their willingness to learn these skills and provide knowledge as to their effectiveness, have allowed us the opportunity to develop, refine, and revise these texts.

We would also like to acknowledge the individual instructors who taught the first group of students from these texts, and gave willingly of their time and talents in the development of this series.

These initial instructors were Arthur Dell Orto, Marianne Farkas, Robert Lasky, Patrice Muchowske, Paul Power, Don Shrey and LeRoy Spaniol.

Particular appreciation is expressed to Marianne Farkas, who not only taught these skills, but who also assisted in the editing and evaluation of these training texts.

Boston, Massachusetts

W.A.A.

M.R.C.

R.M.P.

THE SKILLS OF DIAGNOSTIC PLANNING

Chapter 1 *THE DIAGNOSTIC PLANNING MODEL*

Stated most broadly, the goal of psychiatric rehabilitation is to restore to clients their capacity to function in the community. Philosophically, this means that rehabilitation is directed at increasing the *strengths* of the clients so that they can achieve their maximum potential for independent living and meaningful careers. Although many traditional treatment approaches seek to prepare clients to function independently, the emphasis in traditional psychiatric treatment has typically been on the reduction of client discomfort by changing underlying personality structures, increasing client insights, and alleviating symptomatology. The emphasis in psychiatric rehabilitation is on understanding the clients' problems in living in terms of "skill deficits." Although psychiatric rehabilitation shares with traditional psychiatric treatment the mission of helping psychiatrically disabled clients terminate their distress, it distinguishes itself from traditional treatment by emphasizing helping clients to learn the skills which they can apply to real life situations. In essence, the focus of psychiatric rehabilitation is on teaching clients to function effectively in their lives.

Although the total treatment process for disabled psychiatric clients includes both aspects of traditional psychiatric treatment and psychiatric rehabilitation, it is important that these activities be separated conceptually so that the rehabilitation process receives the emphasis necessary to develop its own unique contribution to client care.

This book represents one of a series of books whose purpose is to define and teach the unique skills of psychiatric rehabilitation. The particular skill with which this book is concerned is that of *diagnostic planning*.

THE DEFINITION, PURPOSE AND APPLICATIONS OF DIAGNOSTIC PLANNING

WHAT DIAGNOSTIC PLANNING IS

Diagnostic planning refers to the *interviewing* and *assessment* process by which the rehabilitation practitioner explores the client's strengths and deficits, understands how these strengths and deficits affect the client's ability to function in specific environments, and assesses in an objective manner the level of client skills in relation to what the client needs to function in these specific environments. The outcome of diagnostic planning is a comprehensive picture of the strengths and deficits of the psychiatrically disabled client that implies a rehabilitation plan. The practitioner achieves this diagnostic out-

1

come when the practitioner and client have been able to identify those observable client strengths and weaknesses that affect the client's ability to achieve the specific rehabilitation goals. The purpose of such a rehabilitation diagnosis is to improve the efficacy of treatment services eventually provided to the client.

WHY DIAGNOSTIC PLANNING IS IMPORTANT

Obviously, unique rehabilitation plans cannot be developed and implemented effectively unless a rehabilitation diagnosis of the client is first made. Simply stated, differential treatment requires differential diagnostic assessment.

Because of the rehabilitation practitioner's diagnostic emphasis on skills and skill deficits, the rehabilitation diagnostic plan is strikingly different from the outcome of a typical psychiatric diagnosis. In contrast to the latter type of diagnosis, the rehabilitation diagnostic plan neither attempts to label the psychiatrically disabled client nor to categorize the client's symptomatology. Rather, the rehabilitation diagnostic process yields information about the disabled client's level of skills and the skill demands of the community in which the client wants or needs to function. Such information will enable the rehabilitation practitioner to work with the client to develop a rehabilitation plan designed to increase or more effectively utilize the client's strengths and assets. Implementation of this plan will, in turn, lead to an improved ability on the part of the client to reach his or her rehabilitation goals.

In developing a rehabilitation diagnosis, it is critical to recognize that the client must *accept the diagnosis as valid,* because the client will later be expected to take action based upon an understanding of his or her present functioning. Traditional psychiatric diagnosis has not deliberately emphasized procedures for getting the client to accept the diagnosis nor has it focused on getting the client to understand the diagnosis. Unlike a rehabilitation intervention, however, meaningful psychiatric treatment *can* proceed without prior client acceptance and understanding of the diagnostic label.

In essence, the use of rehabilitation diagnostic planning skills (rather than simple reliance on the techniques of the traditional psychiatric diagnostic assessment) is necessary because of two fundamental facts: (1) the present psychiatric diagnostic categories simply do not provide much input relevant to rehabilitation outcome; and (2) it is the presence or absence of specific skill behaviors, not symptom patterns, that relates to rehabilitation outcome (research summarized in Anthony, 1979).

The fact that a psychiatric diagnosis does not predict rehabilitation outcome is really not that surprising. The psychiatric diagnostic system was developed for the purpose of categorizing symptom patterns, not to provide information relevant to a client's rehabilitation potential. We should not be surprised that the present psychiatric diagnostic system is unable to do something for which it was *not* developed. In addition, controversy still exists concerning whether or not the psychiatric diagnostic system is able to do what it *was* developed to do. In particular, questions have been raised with respect to that diagnostic system's reliability and/or validity. These possible difficulties within the present diagnostic system could pose further problems for the field of psychiatric rehabilitation if practitioners in that field were to rely solely on the diagnostic system created for psychiatric treatment.

In summary, it is the client's unique pattern of strengths and weaknesses that most affect rehabilitation success; therefore, it makes sense to interview for and assess the client's present level of skills and to identify those skills that the client will need in order to function more effectively in the community. In other words, a diagnosis of the client's present and required level of skills provides a direct prognosis of the client's rehabilitation potential. In contrast, the present psychiatric diagnostic system provides information of only limited prognostic value for rehabilitation practitioners. *Thus, because the purpose and outcome of the rehabilitation diagnostic planning process is drastically different from the purpose and outcome of the psychiatric diagnostic process, the specific practitioner skills needed to achieve this rehabilitation diagnostic plan are also dramatically different.*

WHEN AND WHERE DIAGNOSTIC PLANNING CAN BE USED

Diagnostic planning is a necessary skill for anyone who is working with or preparing to work with psychiatric clients in order to assist them in living, learning, and/or working more independently. Diagnostic planning can be used effectively with any psychiatrically disabled client — inpatient or outpatient. The only limitation involves those clients who are so severely disabled that they cannot verbally interact with the practitioner; here the interview component of the diagnostic planning process would need to be adjusted to emphasize observations of the client's nonverbal behavior and verbal input from significant others. It should also be pointed out that diagnostic planning for rehabilitation purposes is seen as appropriate at any time during the psychiatric treatment process. Such planning can occur prior to psychiatric therapy, concurrently with the therapeutic process, or even after the therapeutic process has been completed. The determining criterion is the point at which it becomes functional for the practitioner and the client to understand the skill strengths and deficits that are affecting or will affect the client's attainment of rehabilitation goals.

Rehabilitation diagnosis is ordinarily begun whenever the client is referred for rehabilitation services. There are two basic reasons for a rehabilitation referral: (1) to facilitate the client's ability to remain in her or his present environment; and/or (2) to facilitate the client's ability to function in an environment different from his or her present environment. The major task of the rehabilitation intervention is to teach the client the additional skills that will be needed to function in the environment and/or to modify the environment so as to make it more accommodating to the client's level of ability.

In each of these situations, diagnostic planning should precede the client's learning of new skills and/or the modification of the client's environment. In situations in which the client's environment is changed, the diagnostic planning process can provide an exceptionally helpful amount of information related to the type of environmental setting that is needed. (The one possible exception to the diagnostic planning process as a prerequisite for rehabilitation intervention is the crisis situation in which the client must move to a new environment immediately. Some of the critical practitioner skills necessary to deal with this crisis situation are called "community coordinating" skills and are presented in Book 6 in this series.)

THE STAGES AND SKILLS OF DIAGNOSTIC PLANNING

Since this entire text focuses on how diagnostic planning is accomplished, this section will simply overview the basic stages of diagnostic planning.

The overall *goal* of rehabilitation diagnostic planning is the development of an observable, objective picture of the client's strengths and deficits with respect to the client's initial problem and rehabilitation goal. This diagnostic plan also includes an analysis of any environmental modifications that need to be made in order to assist the client in overcoming his or her situational problem.

Table 1 is an example of a completed Client Diagnostic Planning Chart for one particular client. The top of the chart specifies the particular problem for which the client is being referred or seeking help. In this case, Ms. Smith has been placed in the community but has remained isolated and alone. Her rehabilitation goal is to overcome this isolation by increasing the amount of interaction between herself and other residents in her community. The physical, emotional, and intellectual skills relevant to this rehabilitation goal are identified on the chart. The skills are identified as strengths (+) or deficits (-), depending on how well Ms. Smith is able to perform these skills in relation to the level of functioning she will need in order to achieve her rehabilitation goal. Because the situational problem is only related to Ms. Smith's living environment, Ms. Smith's skills critical to success in either a learning and/or working environment have not been diagnosed.

By examining Ms. Smith's diagnosis, we can envision a woman

Table 1.

Client Diagnostic Planning Chart

CLIENT DIAGNOSTIC PLANNING CHART   Name ___Ms. Smith___

Situational Problem: Does not interact with anyone in her neighborhood.

Rehabilitation Goal: Increase amount of interaction between Ms. Smith and community residents.

Environment	Strength / Deficit	Physical Skills	Emotional Skills	Intellectual Skills
Living apartment and neighborhood	+	Housework Grooming Driving a car Using public transportation	Listening	Budgeting Shopping Cooking
	–	Physical fitness	Conversing Telephoning	Scheduling time Identifying interests Goal setting Decision making
Learning	+			
	–			
Working	+			
	–			

who seems to be able to function independently in her apartment (i.e., she possesses the skills necessary for apartment upkeep). The deficits that have been diagnosed suggest those behaviors that can be focused on in order to improve her ability to interact in the community.

Once the critical skills related to the rehabilitation goal have been diagnosed, the rehabilitation diagnostician must also define exactly what each skill means for that particular client. For Ms. Smith's situation, for example, the skill of identifying interests might mean "increasing from zero to five the number of activities that Ms. Smith considers potentially satisfying to her."

The rehabilitation practitioner develops this type of diagnostic picture for each presenting problem. Examples of some of the more typical rehabilitation problems are: no job-goal or unrealistic job-goal, no job, no job-skills, inability to adjust to a work or school setting, no place to live, overly dependent on medication, unable to follow medication schedule, unable to get along with housemates, and no environmental support system.

In order to achieve the comprehensive diagnostic picture necessary to develop rehabilitation plans for such problems as those, the rehabilitation practitioner will want to take the client through the *three fundamental stages* of the diagnostic planning process. These stages are developmental in nature in that the earlier stages must be completed before the later stages can be successfully implemented.

The *first stage* of diagnostic planning is the *exploration* stage. In this initial step, the rehabilitation practitioner attempts to involve the client in an exploration of his or her unique situation and problems and the feelings the client experiences in relation to these situational problems and rehabilitation goals. The *second stage* of diagnostic planning is characterized by the rehabilitation practitioner's efforts to help the client focus on his or her own role in the rehabilitation process; the aim is to promote the client's *understanding* of the ways in which his or her unique strengths and weaknesses may be a help or hindrance in achieving the rehabilitation goals. In the *third stage* of the diagnostic planning process, the rehabilitation practitioner *assesses* in observable, measurable terms the client's present and needed level of skills-based behavior needed to overcome the individual's situational problems.

Each of the three stages outlined above requires specific practitioner skills. These stages and their skills are presented in Table 2. In the exploration stage of diagnostic planning, the rehabilitation practitioner uses specific skills to facilitate the client's exploration of his or her unique situation. First, the practitioner seeks to involve the client in the rehabilitation process by *informing* and *encouraging* the client to appear for rehabilitation services. In addition, the rehabilitation practitioner will want to *observe* the client's skills and nonverbal behavior and *listen* to the client's verbal expressions. By using these attending, observing, and listening skills, the rehabilitation practitioner will be

Table 2. The Stages and Skills of Diagnostic Planning

I. EXPLORING THE CLIENT'S UNIQUE PROBLEMS AND GOALS

- A.   Inform and encourage the client to become involved.
- B.   Attend to the client's presence.
- C.   Observe the client's nonverbal behavior and appearance.
- D.   Listen to the client's verbal expressions.
- E.   Respond to the client's verbal and nonverbal expressions.
- F.   Specify the client's situational problems and rehabilitation goals.

II. UNDERSTANDING THE CLIENT'S PERSONAL STRENGTHS AND DEFICITS

- A.   Personalize the meaning of the client's exploration.
- B.   Personalize the client's specific strengths and deficits.
- C.   Categorize the client's strengths and deficits by skill areas.
- D.   Categorize the client's strengths and deficits by environmental areas.

III. ASSESSING THE CLIENT'S PERSONAL STRENGTHS AND DEFICITS

- A.   Operationalize each important strength and deficit.
- B.   Quantify the client's present levels of functioning.
- C.   Quantify the client's needed levels of functioning.

more able to *respond* accurately to the client's verbal and nonverbal expression. The practitioner's ability to respond (i.e., to demonstrate that the practitioner can understand the client's situation) will encourage the client to explore this situation in greater and more relevant detail so that the client and practitioner can accurately *specify* the situational problem and rehabilitation goal.

In the understanding stage of diagnostic planning, the practitioner helps the client move from an exploration of the situation to an understanding of his or her personal strengths and deficits. Once again, specific practitioner skills are needed to facilitate the client's understanding. First, the practitioner will want to *personalize the meaning* of the client's self-exploration (i.e., get the client to discuss the personal implications of the situations that the client has been exploring). The practitioner will also want to *personalize the client's specific strengths and deficits* (i.e., help the client understand his or her unique personal assets and liabilities in relation to the rehabilitation goals). In addition, the practitioner can help the client develop a comprehensive and understandable diagnostic picture of the client's strengths and deficits by *categorizing his or her strengths and deficits by skill areas* (i.e., by indicating whether the client strengths and deficits identified are primarily physical, emotional, and/or intellectual skills). Finally, the practitioner will want to complete the diagnostic picture by *categorizing the client's strengths and deficits by environmental areas* (i.e., determining which specific living, learning, and/or working environments will be affected by the previously identified client strengths and deficits). By using these skills of the second phase of the diagnostic planning process, the rehabilitation practitioner can increase the client's understanding of his or her personal role in the rehabilitation effort.

In the third or assessment stage of the diagnostic planning process, the practitioner objectively assesses the client's previously identified relevant strengths and deficits. In order to undertake this assessment, the practitioner needs certain skills. First, the practitioner will need to *operationalize each strength and deficit* (i.e., to write a descriptive statement of the strength or deficit in terms that allow the strength or deficit to be observed). In most instances the practitioner will also need the expertise necessary to *quantify the client's present and needed levels of functioning* with respect to each environmental area of interest. The discrepancies between the client's present and needed levels of functioning invariably suggest the specific type of rehabilitation treatment intervention that will be needed.

The remainder of this text provides the details related to the three diagnostic planning stages and the practitioner skills necessary to develop a diagnostic plan. The complexity of the diagnostic planning process will vary depending upon the needs of the client and the rehabilitation referral request. It is important, however, that the practitioner master the diagnostic planning skills necessary to deal with the most complex situation. In this way, the practitioner will possess the skills necessary to deal with the entire range of rehabilitation referrals and the client needs.

Chapter 2 *EXPLORING THE CLIENT'S UNIQUE SITUATIONAL PROBLEMS AND REHABILITATION GOALS*

EXPLORING: AN UNSKILLED APPROACH

Paul opened the door to the outer office. "Uh — listen, Stella, you did say that the appointment for Mary Thorne was set for three this afternoon, didn't you?"

"Absolutely!" Picking up a postal-type card from a pile on the corner of her desk, Stella turned from her typewriter and offered the card to Paul. "I sent her a regular card about the appointment — just like always."

Paul took the card and looked at it idly. On the front side the return address of his office was preprinted; Stella always typed in the name and address of new clients. On the reverse side was a preprinted message that certainly seemed to Paul to be simple, clear, and to the point. It said:

> *Mr./Mrs./Miss _____ has an appointment with Paul Gervasi at _____ A.M./P.M. on _____ Please be prompt.*
>
> *Paul Gervasi*
> *Thornwood Clinic*
> *23 Saratoga Way*
> *Weymouth, Mass.*
> *(617) 455-9880*

What could be easier to understand? Whenever a new client was referred to Paul, Stella filled in the appropriate information on the back of one of the cards, addressed it, and sent it off. No fuss, no muss, no confusion. Why then did so many of these new clients never appear?

Stella was obviously wondering the same thing. Paul could see it in her eyes. Her thought was as clear as his own: "Well, there's another no-show, huh?"

Another one. Like Charley Johnson, the guy referred to Paul by the VA Hospital. Like Mavis Springer. Like the numerous others who existed only as faceless names on a list of unkept appointments.

Why? Wherever he turned, Paul kept running into this insistent question. Why, why, why? For God's sake, he was a professional doing a professional's job, wasn't he? Didn't these people know that he wanted to help them — that he could help them? Didn't they know that the time he spent waiting for them was valuable time? Didn't they want or even appreciate what he was prepared to do for them?

Several minutes later, Paul was still struggling with the same questions when Stella stuck her head in the door.

"Hey, I got Mary Thorne's phone number and called her," she told Paul. "She said other things came up and she couldn't make it today. She'll give us a call to set up another time."

"She'll give us a call ..." Paul turned away, not wanting to meet Stella's concerned gaze. "Okay, thanks ..."

*He heard the door close softly behind him. What **was** it with these people, anyway? For crying out loud, they acted like they weren't even **involved** — and all the time it was their lives that Paul was trying to put back together!*

Trying, yes — but not accomplishing. Paul could have promoted the appearance of new clients in many ways: by letting them know the purpose of their appointment; by letting them know some real ways in which he could help them; by letting them know just how to get to his office; by *encouraging* their appearance.

But Paul's preprinted announcement concerning each appointment was far too brief, cold, and uninviting. It did not encourage — it discouraged! And for this reason, many new clients simply did not make the effort required to get to their appointments.

Getting clients to appear for rehabilitation certainly does not insure that they will return for additional treatment and explore in detail their unique rehabilitation situations, of course. Lucy Amos, a counselor at a rehabilitation agency, was exceptionally successful in getting her clients to show up for their first appointments. Yet as the following story suggests, Lucy was not similarly successful in eliciting self-exploration from the clients whom she saw.

"How come you gotta know all this stuff about my school and family and like that? Isn't it all right there in my file?"

Lucy looked up from the file on her desk and regarded the girl sitting across from her. The girl, Jen Pinchot, stared back at Lucy without blinking.

"Yes, Jen, most of this information is in the file. But I often find it helpful to hear clients talk about their background in their own words."

Jen glared at her. "Then how come you just sit there with your nose in the file all the time I'm talking?"

Lucy sighed and leaned back in her chair. "Do you enjoy pushing people like that, Jen?" she asked. "Is that how things turned sour for you in college? Because you kept pushing at people? Quite frankly, I'm not surprised."

"You don't know a damned thing about it!" Jen exclaimed heatedly. Lucy ignored her comment and pursued her own train of thought.

"According to your file, you were doing just fine. Good grades, good reports, everything going well. Then, just before your — breakdown — you apparently stopped doing any work at all. I want to know why."

"You want to know why?" Jen was obviously furious. She fumbled a cigarette out of her pocketbook and lit it. "I'll tell you why. Because all the people at the stupid college turned out to be just like you, that's why!"

Again, Lucy ignored the outburst. She felt that any recognition of such behavior only gave the individual involved the attention he or she wanted. No point in rewarding people for their own irrationality. Instead, swiveling her chair to present her profile to the angry girl, she framed another question. "You were in the hospital almost three months, weren't you? Do you think the experience was helpful at all?"

Unnoticed by Lucy, Jen shuddered at the mention of the word "hospital." She looked down at the smoldering end of her cigarette. "Sure it helped — the same way prisons help reform people!"

Lucy sighed again. She really felt it was too soon for her to be able to help this girl. Perhaps what Jen needed most was a longer period of time to adjust to life back with her family. She would calm down eventually. Lucy felt sure of that. Turning front again, she tried to smile in a friendly fashion.

"I think maybe we're trying to rush things," she said. "Let's set up another appointment for — oh, maybe next Thursday. Okay?"

Jen's only response was a shrug. Lucy got up and walked with Jen to the door. "My secretary will set up the appointment for you."

Jen didn't look at her. "Yeah, sure," she muttered, the corners of her mouth turned down in a grimace. "See you . . ."

Before clients can begin to explore their unique rehabilitation situation, they must first *appear* for treatment. To some, it might seem that the clients' appearance would be a foregone conclusion. After all, it is the clients who benefit from rehabilitation services — why shouldn't they want to come? However, there is evidence to suggest that client appearance at an interview is far from an automatic process, as we saw in the brief account that began this chapter. For example, one study indicated that approximately *two-thirds* of the clients referred from a psychiatric hospital to a community-based rehabilitation center failed to appear (Wolkon, 1970)! From the client's perspective, the present referral system may seem more like a "dumping" system than a referral system.

It would appear that rehabilitation practitioners must do more than simply make appointments with psychiatrically disabled clients. The client needs to be specifically informed and encouraged to appear for rehabilitation. No-shows are not just clients who no longer need or want rehabilitation services. In fact, some of the no-shows may be the clients who are most in need of rehabilitation intervention. The rehabilitation practitioner need not rationalize a client's failure to appear with an argument similar to, "...if they don't want my help, there are plenty of clients that can take their place." Instead, the psychiatric rehabilitation practitioner will want to use additional skills to insure that most rehabilitation clients do appear for treatment. Two of these skills involve *informing* and *encouraging* the psychiatrically disabled client to appear for help.

INFORMING AND ENCOURAGING THE CLIENT TO BECOME INVOLVED

INFORMING

Informing a client about an interview in such a manner that the client is likely to appear may well seem like such a simple skill that it does not even need to be addressed. There are various strategies that the rehabilitation practitioner can use, however, that will maximize the probability of a psychiatrically disabled client appearing for rehabilitation services.

Whether the client is informed in writing, in person, or by phone, the invitation should be based on the six interrogatives, or 5WH strategy. That is, the client should be informed of the details with respect to *who, what, when, where, why,* and *how*. The "who" identifies the practitioner with whom the appointment is scheduled. The "what" tells what will happen (e.g., initial counseling interview). The "where" and "when" simply address the time and place. In terms of place, it may be necessary to go beyond a street address and give a more precise location (e.g., "second floor, third door on the left"). The "how" portion of the invitation deals with how a client gets there. This could involve such general items as a map, personalized directions, or even instructions about what to do upon arrival (e.g., "Report to the receptionist and tell her you have an appointment with me."). The "why" of the invitation looks at the general purpose of the appointment (e.g., "to explore your employment situation").

A written informative invitation for an initial interview might be developed like the one in Table 3. This initial invitation contains all the elements regarding who, what, when, where, how, and why. For an ongoing client, all of this information may not be necessary. An ongoing client, for example, would certainly not need directions. The minimum amount of information that any client should have in advance is the time of the next session and the purpose. The purpose becomes the starting point for the next session. The statement of purpose can also be helpful in evaluating the next session (i.e., Did the session accomplish the agreed-upon purpose or not?).

Table 3. Sample Informative Invitation

Name: _____*John Ross*_____ Today's Date: ___*9/14/79*___

Appointment: _____*Individual Counseling Interview*_____

Purpose: _*To talk about your needs and how the agency might be of*_
_____*service to you.*_____

Appointment Date: _*9/28*_ _*10 a.m.*_ With: _*Mr. Wendell Harris*_

Location: 1400 Main Street, 2nd Floor, Room 207. The receptionist will direct you to Mr. Harris's office. Enclosed you will find a map.

Practice Situations

Below is a brief sketch of a client. Assume that this client has been set up to see you for an initial interview two weeks from now.

Joe Jenning is a twenty-four-year-old male. He was discharged a week ago from the Veterans Hospital. He was referred to your agency by the hospital staff and has called for an appointment. The receptionist made an appointment for you to meet with him at 10:00 A.M., two weeks from today's date.

Use the form in Table 4 to write your invitation for an appointment to Joe.

As an additional practice exercise, choose an actual client that you now have or are about to receive and fill out Table 4 for this client. Be sure to include the purpose of the contact as well as any other information this client needs.

Table 4. Sample Client Invitation Form

Name: _____ Today's Date: _____

Appointment: _____

Purpose: _____

_____

Appointment Date: ____ _____ With: _____

Location: _____

_____

ENCOURAGING

In addition to supplying general information, the invitation should also give the client a personal reason to appear. An invitation encourages the physical appearance of the client if it stresses the specific *benefits* that appearance may bring. In other words, the emphasis should be on one or another version of the familiar "If you contact me, you will learn something to your advantage" approach. Although stating the purpose of the interview takes a step in this direction, encouraging should go a step beyond and give the client some hope of achieving something of personal benefit. In order to accomplish this, the practitioner needs to take something known about the client and give some evidence that the practitioner and/or the agency can be of assistance. The general format is: "I understand that *(information regarding the client's need or desire for services). I (personal expression of interest)."* In essence, the client is encouraged to appear by means of this personal message. For example, to the previous invitation to John Ross the practitioner might have added a personal note encouraging him to appear. Such a note is shown in Table 5.

It is clear that encouragement is critical to ensure the client appears for the first interview. An additional source of encouragement can be a phone-call reminder several days before the scheduled appointment. After that, encouragement will frequently be a factor of the productivity of the previous session. Even in ongoing sessions, however, it may be necessary to recognize the client's reaction to the interview and use this reaction as the information with which to encourage him or her to appear at the next session.

Table 5. Sample Informative and Encouraging Invitation

Name: _____*John Ross*_____ Today's Date: ___*9/14*___

Appointment: _____*Individual Counseling Interview*_____

Purpose: *To talk about your needs and how the agency might be of* _____ *service to you.*_____

Appointment Date: ___*9/28 10 a.m.*___ With: ___*Mr. Wendell Harris*___

Location: 1400 Main Street, 2nd Floor, Room 207. The receptionist will direct you to Mr. Harris's office. Enclosed you will find a map.

NOTE: Mr. Ross: I understand that you have been referred to us by Dr. Brown. She informs me that you are beginning to feel restless and are eager to try working again. I will look forward to seeing you and discussing what some of your first steps might be.

14

Practice Situations

As an initial practice exercise, add a personal note to the previous invitation that you wrote for Joseph Henning (Table 4).

Now add a personal note to the invitation you developed earlier for one of your own ongoing clients. The encouragement can be based on what the client has accomplished or something that you know he or she wants to accomplish in relation to the general purpose of the session.

As a final step, develop your own personal informative invitation and begin sending it to the clients whom you will be seeing in the next several weeks. Make sure that your invitation answers the six basic interrogatives.

INFORMING AND ENCOURAGING: A SUMMARY

Goal: To maximize the possibility that the client will appear for service.

1. Identify the mode of communication (written, telephone, in person).

2. Identify the amount of information the client needs (who, what, when, where, and how).

3. Identify the purpose of the appointment (why).

4. Identify the specific benefits of the appointment to the client.

5. Issue the invitation to the client.

6. If necessary, several days before the scheduled appointment, contact the client again as a reminder of the appointment.

ATTENDING TO THE CLIENT'S PRESENCE

Getting the client to put in an appearance is an obvious first step toward enabling the client to explore his or her situation. However, the practitioner will also want to make sure that the client feels enough care and support to wish to continue in treatment. Once again, just as we noted difficulties involved in getting clients to appear for help, many clients choose to terminate treatment prematurely. Garfield (1971) has summarized data that indicates that a large number of clients prematurely drop out of counseling and psychotheraphy of their own volition. A recent study by Sue, McKinney, and Allen (1976) of 13,450 clients seen in nineteen community mental health facilities found that 40 percent of these clients terminated treatment after only one session! Practitioners need to become more aware of various strategies aimed at maximizing the clients' ongoing presence in treatment.

One way to increase a client's involvement in the rehabilitation process is to communicate attention and interest in the client — i.e., to *attend* to the client. Research evidence is available that supports the common-sense notion that people are more willing to express themselves to people who are paying attention to them (Mehrabian, 1972). Furthermore, by attending to clients, practitioners convey the impression that they care for and are listening to the clients. Rehabilitation practitioners can ensure that their psychiatrically disabled clients feel attended to by employing their attending skills. Attending skills include both *contextual attending* and *personal attending*. The former addresses the way in which the environment can be arranged to communicate support. The latter looks at what the practitioner can do personally to communicate interest and attention.

CONTEXTUAL ATTENDING

There are two elements that comprise contextual attending. These include the arrangement of the office furniture and the decorations and materials contained in the office. For a one-to-one diagnostic interview, the furniture often includes two comfortable chairs and a desk or table on which to place any materials that are needed for the interview. The chairs can be placed opposite each other, four to five feet apart with no barriers between them. Diagramatically, the layout might look like this:

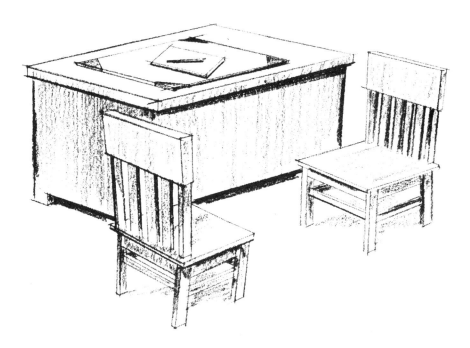

With more than one client, the practitioner can use an arc arrangement of clients' chairs at a 90-degree angle to her or his own seat. If an imaginary line is established from the end of each of the practitioner's shoulders, the chairs would fall within that line. The arrangement might look as follows:

Placing the chairs opposite each other will enable the practitioner to face each client directly. Along with eliminating barriers to a full communication process, this will allow the practitioner to observe the client more fully. A distance of four to five feet is close, yet far enough away so that practitioner and client do not invade each other's personal life space.

When the practitioner's and each client's chairs are of the same or a similar type and of approximately equal height, a sense of equality and partnership is communicated. Traditionally, the message communicated by the furniture selection has been ignored. A survey conducted at the psychiatric facility of one major university found that the practitioners' chairs were always one or two inches higher than the clients'. The practitioner often sat in a large, padded, swivel-type chair while the client was restricted to a small, straight-backed, unpadded, plastic or wooden chair!

If any writing is to be done or materials referred to, the table or desk may be placed to one side with the needed materials on it. "Materials" as used here refer to items that are actually used. "Decorations" refer to items that serve to personalize the office. The purpose of materials and decorations is to facilitate the client's feeling comfortable about expressing himself or herself. Materials that are to be used (e.g., pencils, paper, case records) can be arranged so that the practitioner has easy access to them and does not have to create a commotion trying to find something. Materials that could be potential distractions (e.g., tape recorders or telephones) can be handled in such a way as to minimize their interference. Recorders can be placed under desks rather than right in front of the client; incoming phone calls can be blocked. Materials such as professional books can reflect the kinds of areas and problems with which clients are concerned.

Decorations that reflect the client's own frame of reference make him or her feel welcome. In other words, when the clients look around the office, they can find something familiar to them. This can be a picture, an artifact, or even a book. When the practitioner deals with clients who are demographically unlike himself or herself, this need is heightened. It has frequently been observed that white, middle-class practitioners may have no decorations of any kind with which the minority client can identify. The clients' reaction is often to wonder whether or not they are truly welcome. It is worth noting that one study has found that over 50 percent of black clients terminated treatment after only one contact at community mental health center facilities (Sue, McKinney, Allen & Hall, 1974).

Finally, it is helpful if all the objects in the interview room are clean and orderly. The client seeking help is frequently living in a world that is chaotic. Ordering your interviewing room gives the client a chance to get some respite from this chaos. Just as important, a clean and ordered room communicates that you are in control of your affairs and are able to focus your attention on the clients; that is, they can see that you are not distracted by a clutter of materials and objects around you.

Practice Situations

Below is an interview room that is prepared to receive clients.

Now look at this room.

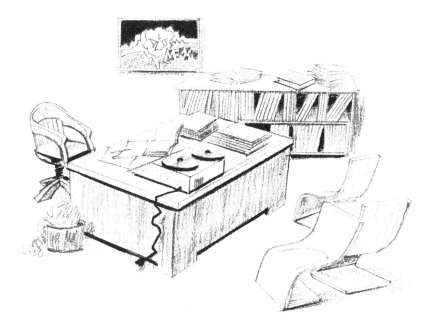

On a separate piece of paper, list the things to be done to prepare the second room for an interview.

Now make a list of things that might be done to your own office in order to prepare it for an interview.

Finally, you may use these suggestions as a basis for actually preparing your office to receive your clients.

PERSONAL ATTENDING

As with contextual attending, the goal of personal attending is to facilitate the client's expressions by having the practitioner communicate interest and attention. There are two components involved for the practitioner: meeting the client's immediate physical needs, and taking a physical posture to communicate attentiveness.

Occasionally, there are very real physical needs that must be met before a client can get involved in a diagnostic interview — the client may have no place to live, may not have eaten in several days, or may be so agitated that she or he has been unable to sleep and has reached a point of exhaustion. In such cases the practitioner must obviously help the client meet these needs so that the client can later become involved in the interviewing process. The rehabilitation practitioner can use community coordinating skills to resolve crisis situations such as these.

19

In most cases, however, the typical physical needs the practitioner addresses are those things that will help clients to be physically comfortable at the moment (e.g., comfortable chairs to sit on, a place to put their coats, a comfortable room temperature). In addition, it may be appropriate to offer clients coffee, tea, or some other form of symbolic nourishment to help them relax.

Once basic physical needs have been addressed, the practitioner is ready to position himself or herself for the diagnostic interview. Communicating interest and attention through one's posture involves five specific behaviors: establishing a proper distance, facing squarely, inclining toward the client, maintaining eye contact, and eliminating distracting behavior.

A good deal of experimental evidence does exist that shows that an interviewer's posture does influence the interviewee's perceptions of the interviewer's ability to be warm and understanding (Genther & Moughan, 1977; Smith-Hanen, 1977).

An illustration showing the correct attending posture is shown below. By establishing a comfortable distance of about four feet, the practitioner is close enough to the client to minimize outside distractions and to observe and hear the most subtle cues expressed by the client. At the same time, this is far enough away so that the client will not feel that his or her personal life space has been violated.

Besides establishing the proper distance, the practitioner will also want to face the client squarely. This means the practitioner's left shoulder is opposite the client's right shoulder and vice versa. By facing the client fully, the practitioner communicates full attentiveness to the client. In addition, this puts the practitioner in the best position to be able to observe the client.

A third dimension in positioning to communicate attention is to incline oneself toward the client. When sitting, as in the picture shown earlier, the practitioner is fully inclined when his forearms can rest comfortably on the thighs. By assuming a forward-leaning posture similar to this, the practitioner communicates full involvement. In general, whenever we are interested in something, we tend to lean toward it.

A fourth aspect of positioning for attending is to develop eye contact with the client. This is also portrayed in the earlier picture. Eye contact accomplishes two things. First, it is a key nonverbal behavior in establishing a link between two people. Second, the face is the place where the most nonverbal cues can be observed. Developing and maintaining eye contact does not mean a staring contest. Rather, it means that the practitioner will want to spend most of the time looking at the face of the client. If the client needs to duck the head or even turn away for a moment of privacy, so be it. The practitioner should, however, continue to reach out to the client by looking at him or her.

The fifth component of attending is to eliminate distracting behaviors. Although the practitioner does not have to sit like a statue, it is important to not be constantly fidgeting. By planting both feet on the floor and holding his hands still, the practitioner in the earlier picture helps to eliminate the distracting movements of his hands or feet. Again, this is not to say that one cannot cross one's legs or use one's hands to talk. Hand gestures can certainly be used to emphasize what the practitioner is saying. The hands and feet should be still when the client is talking so that no impatience is communicated.

Aside from "fidgeting" behaviors, the practitioner will also want to be careful not to be distracting to the client in terms of dress and grooming. Wild hairstyles and "way-out" clothes may make it difficult for the client to focus on what the practitioner is saying. In addition, to the extent that the dress and grooming of the practitioner is something that clients find unfamiliar and foreign, the clients will feel less free to express themselves.

In short, the practitioner is there to serve the client and, therefore, all behaviors are aimed at promoting a positive interaction with the client. These simple attending postures initially convince many clients that you do care and are listening to them. As a practitioner, however, you may feel awkward positioning yourself in the manner described. Remember that anything new seems awkward. With the psychiatrically disabled client, however, the communication of interest should be as clear and full as possible.

Yet the client, too, may initially feel somewhat afraid of the intense attention. Many people — and again this is especially true of the psychiatrically disabled client —associate attention with negative attention. Although one alternative would be for the practitioner to decrease the intensity of attending behaviors, a second alternative is to help the client work through the problem. The reason for choosing the second alternative is that the practitioner needs to focus intense attention on the client in order to obtain the cues needed to make an effective diagnosis. In addition, attending does lead to client expression. Beyond this, of course, it is an opportunity for the client to learn that constructive attention does exist. Also, it has been our observation that most practitioners err on the side of communicating too little attention rather than too much. Finally, if the practitioner cannot work through this relatively minor problem with the client, there is little chance of establishing enough of a relationship to conduct an effective diagnostic interview and to help the client reach the rehabilitation goals.

Practice Situations

Take a moment and develop an attending position with an imaginary client. Place the chairs where they need to be and then assume an attending position. Check yourself on the following questions:

	YES	NO
Were the chairs four to five feet apart?		
Did you face the other chair squarely?		
Did you lean far enough forward so that your forearms could rest on your knees?		
Did you look at where the client's face would be?		
Did you sit still and eliminate distracting behaviors?		

Now practice attending while you are in a regular conversation. Do you notice others expressing themselves more when you are positioning for attending as opposed to turning away? Finally, practice your attending behaviors with your clients — both by meeting their physical needs and by positioning. Note their reaction to your attending. For now, if you notice your current clients becoming uncomfortable because this is a drastic change from your typical interviewing posture, you may have to reduce the intensity of your attending behavior.

ATTENDING: A SUMMARY

Goal: To maximize the possibility of the client continuing in treatment.

1. Arrange office furniture, decorations, and materials to reflect interest in treatment.

2. If necessary, attend to the clients physical needs.

3. Posture oneself for attending by:
   a. establishing the correct distance,
   b. facing the client squarely,
   c. inclining toward the client,
   d. maintaining eye contact,
   e. refraining from distracting movements.

OBSERVING THE CLIENT'S NONVERBAL BEHAVIOR AND APPEARANCE

Attending skills, besides helping the client to feel cared for and supported, are also important because of their critical relationship to the *observing* skills of the practitioner. This relationship between practitioner attending and observing skills is apparent in several key ways. First, an attentive posture and environment facilitates observing by reducing the observer's possible distractions and increasing the ability to focus on the client. Second, by making observations of the client's own attending posture, the practitioner can obtain data from which to draw possible inferences about the client's feeling-state and energy level. Third, paying attention to clients can make them more nonverbally expressive and thus increase the amount of nonverbal information available to the practitioner. An excellent source of a number of experiments on nonverbal behavior —some of which are related to the previous three points —as well as a review of pertinent literature on subjects related to attending and observing can be found in Mehrabian (1972).

The rehabilitation diagnostic planning process requires that a practitioner be skilled in observing. Psychiatrically disabled clients often exhibit incongruities between *what* they say and *how* they say it. Other clients are capable of communicating more information about themselves nonverbally than they are verbally. Accurate observational skills are critically important throughout the diagnostic planning process because they facilitate the practitioner's attempts at assessing the client's degree of skilled behavior in various real or simulated settings.

Many practitioners tend to think of observation as a natural and automatic capability. Yet we are often far less observant than we think —a fact that is true even among those whose profession emphasizes observing skills.

Consider the following real-life situation, which occurred during an in-service training program for experienced police officers. During one class period, a senior police administrator lectured to the assembled officers on the importance of visual observation. By previous arrangement, a young man slipped quietly into the room in the middle of the lecture. This man had a mustache, long hair in a ponytail, was slender and about six-feet tall, and wore blue coveralls with the legend "ACE WINDOW SERVICE" on the back. Without interrupting the lecture, he crossed behind the speaker and proceeded to wash the large window. Having performed this task, he left as quietly as he had come.

At this point, the speaker abruptly halted his lecture and asked each of his "students" to write out a brief description of the person who had just spent some five minutes in full view of the class. Of the sixteen police officers in the class, eight identified the visitor as a woman, three others omitted any reference to his large, droopy mustache, and only one recalled the legend on the back of his coveralls. Even worse, seven officers were unable to specify any task he had performed while most of the others indicated he had done things like "empty wastebaskets" and "move chairs around." In the end, not one of the sixteen experienced police officers was able to give anything approaching an accurate description of the visitor and his actions while in the room!

Obviously, the often-subtle changes in appearance and behavior, which contribute to an accurate diagnosis of a client, are even more difficult to observe. In addition, ours has become a world so focused on words that the significant cues to a client's unique frame of reference that can be derived from observations of physical behavior and appearance are frequently passed over. It is as if the practitioner were moving too quickly to really stop and see the client.

In addition to being a very skilled process, observation is also a very purposive, deliberate process that is directed at ends beyond the simple act of observation itself. The purpose of observation is to secure material that will play a role in the diagnostic planning process. In other words, there are specific variables for which the practitioner observes during the diagnostic planning process. The three main areas that seem to be most critical to later rehabilitation efforts —and from which much can be learned by skillful observing — are the client's *energy level,* the client's *feelings* about specific people and events, and the client's *skill* strengths and weaknesses.

OBSERVING FOR ENERGY LEVEL

Energy level is one of the keys to understanding an individual's functioning and frame of reference. When energy is high, one is more apt to function at one's best. Energy enables the individual to follow through on achieving goals in the face of adverse circumstances and to experience the fullness of life. When an individual's energy is low, it is much easier to feel discouraged and burdened by the demands of life. In short, the client's energy level will affect his or her ability to achieve desired rehabilitation goals. Therefore, this energy level represents important diagnostic information that the practitioner can obtain.

In making observations about energy level, the practitioner may ask and answer the following question: "What does this feature of the client's behavior or appearance tell me about his or her energy level?" Four specific areas on which to concentrate in making observations about energy level are *body build, posture, grooming,* and *nonverbal expressions.* Observations in each area can be tied to specific and objectively verifiable visual cues (e.g., "she's five-foot-five, about one-hundred-sixty pounds" as opposed to "she's too heavy"; "he wears clean, tailored clothes" as opposed to "he's a sharp dresser").

In terms of *body build,* the practitioner can begin by asking these questions: "Clothes and grooming aside, how can I describe this client's physical appearance?"; or "What is his/her height and weight and are they in proportion?"; or "How muscular is the client?" In general, the more muscular the client and the better proportioned in terms of height and weight, the better the energy level.

Posture refers to the way in which the client holds his or her body. The practitioner can ask and answer the question: "What is the shape of the client's body when sitting or standing and what does this imply about energy level (e.g., alertness)?" Specifically, the practitioner will look for the same cues that were discussed earlier in practitioner attending. Thus, alertness and energy are suggested by the extent to which the client sits and stands erect or is inclined forward with eyes focused on the practitioner. The client who sits slouched in the seat with shoulders drooping is taking a posture suggestive of a low level of energy.

Grooming as used here encompasses both mode of dress and personal hygiene. Again, the practitioner may begin by asking a question: "What does the client's dress and personal hygiene suggest about his or her level of energy?" In general, cleanliness and neatness suggest at least an adequate level of energy. More elaborate dress and grooming would suggest that looks are not only important to the client but that he or she has a high enough level of energy to be able to invest effort in this area. In contrast, a disheveled and unkempt appearance, though perhaps merely showing disregard for the area of personal grooming, could also reflect the fact that the client is disabled to the point of having little energy to invest in taking care of him or herself.

Finally, there are *nonverbal expressions* from which inferences of energy level can be developed. Ample evidence exists to show that the various ways in which people move their bodies and faces reflect a good deal about what these people are feeling and thinking; however, it cannot be assumed that any complete and standardized "vocabulary" of nonverbal expressions exists. Different people express themselves in different ways. For example, most Westerners indicate agreement by nodding the head up and down. Many people in Asian societies, however, indicate just the opposite (complete disagreement) by using the same head motion.

In inferring the meaning of nonverbal expressions, then, the practitioner will again want to use caution. The question to ask here is: "What is this person doing that might be seen as an indicator of energy level?" Such things as slow movements, slumped shoulders, and a slack face are frequently suggestive of a low level of energy.

In drawing any inference from observational cues, the rehabilitation practitioner will want to realize that the purpose of such observational inferences is not to encourage the practitioner to make quick diagnostic judgments about the client. Rather, the purpose is to systematically use the nonverbal behavior and appearance of the client as a source of diagnostic *hypotheses* to be confirmed or denied by the ongoing interaction with the client. In communicating with other professionals about a client's level of functioning, it is important for practitioners to be able to distinguish between observations and inferences based on observations.

OBSERVING FOR FEELINGS

These same four areas of body build, posture, grooming, and nonverbal expression may be used as aids in diagnosing the client's *feelings* as well as energy level. *Feelings* are simply the affective reactions the client has to his or her situation. At a gross level, the client can feel good, bad, or indifferent. These gross categories of feeling can be broken down into subareas. One effective way of grouping feelings would be: happy, angry, sad, confused, scared, strong, and weak. Each of these feeling-states may be experienced by a client at high, moderate, and low intensities. In observing for feelings, the practitioner can ask and answer the question: "What does this feature of the client's body build, posture, grooming, and nonverbal expression tell me about the client's feelings?"

Although nonverbal expressions are perhaps the richest source of data concerning the feelings of the client, the other areas also can contribute to the practitioner's diagnosis. Poor grooming, for example, may well be reflective of a "down feeling." At another level, a large, strong male may be more prone to feelings of shame at the "weakness" that his disability implies. Finally, a client's posture in relation to the practitioner may say a great deal about the way in which the client feels about the practitioner.

Observing the degree of congruence in the client's behavior and appearance can give the practitioner additional cues from which energy levels and feelings can be inferred. Client "congruence" simply refers to the degree to which the client exhibits no obvious discrepancies or incongruities. One example of client incongruity is the large, well-muscled individual (connoting high energy) whose body build is at odds with his slow, listless behavior and slouched posture (connoting low energy). The inference from these conflicting energy indicators could be that the client has an enduring high level of energy that is being drained by his present emotion situation. Conflicting aspects of nonverbal behavior and appearance can also give information about client feelings. A client may be sitting up straight in the chair, smiling at the practitioner, but tapping his foot and fidgeting with his fingers. The feeling that can be inferred from this incongruent behavior might be "mixed" feelings, or "nervous and controlled."

OBSERVING FOR SKILLS

Last but by no means least, the practitioner can observe a client's body build, posture, grooming, and nonverbal expressions for cues as to various skills the client possesses. Undoubtedly the major source of data from which inferences about skills can be made is obtained when the practitioner arranges to observe the client outside of the rehabilitation interview setting. By interacting with the client in the client's own environment, the practitioner can make observations on how skillfully the client interacts with the environment. Or by setting up a simulated environment and having the client role-play certain behaviors, the practitioner can also directly observe various skills. However, even in a rehabilitation setting the practitioner can make some skill inferences, particularly with respect to the client's interpersonal skills. Indications of the client's own attending skills, greeting skills, and conversational skills can be obtained by watching how the client interacts with people in the office. Observing possessions that the client brings to the rehabilitation environment can also provide some indication of the client's skills. For example, observations of the client's reading material, dress, and jewelry might provide a data base for some inferences about the client's skill strengths and deficits.

As an example of diagnosing energy levels, feelings, and skills, look at the picture below of a practitioner and her client.

First, looking at *energy level*, it can be seen that the practitioner is a large woman (5′8″ or so, about 145 pounds) with good muscle tone. She is also sitting alertly (inclined forward, looking at the client) and her grooming looks neat and clean. The expression on her face seems "intent" as seen by her steady gaze and relaxed features. These observations are indicative of a high energy level. The client, on the other hand, is a small man (about 5′6″, 140 pounds) whose muscles do not appear well developed. He also does not seem very alert as he sits slumped in his chair. His grooming does seem to be adequately neat and clean. Finally, the expression on the client's face is slack. Altogether, then, this client would seem to have a low *level of energy* — although he still has enough vitality in his daily life to get himself together in terms of grooming.

In terms of *feeling,* the practitioner seems to feel confident and interested as indicated by the fact that she is sitting forward and looking directly at the client with the muscles in her face relaxed. The client looks as if he is feeling "down" as indicated by his slouched posture and slack facial expression. He also seems to have some negative feelings about the relationship with the practitioner as indicated by his turning away with his body and not looking at her.

Finally, the practitioner seems to have a high level of attending skill, physical fitness skills, and grooming skills. In contrast, the picture of the client raises questions about all those skills except for grooming. The client is sitting in a poor attending posture. The poor muscle tone may suggest low levels of fitness. Only in the area of grooming does the client exhibit skill strengths. In summary, the initial inferences and their related observations for this client are presented in Table 6.

By skillfully observing psychiatrically disabled clients, practitioners can become aware of their client's congruence or lack of congruence. As the practitioner looks at the four areas of body build, posture, grooming, and nonverbal expression, she or he can consider, "Are there any two or more behaviors or appearances which are inconsistent with one another?" Many times psychiatrically disabled clients display discrepancies in their behaviors (e.g., sitting erect but eyes closed), discrepancies in their appearance (e.g., dirty hands but clean clothes), or discrepancies between their behavior and their appearance (e.g., dressed in a three piece business suit but sitting slumped and curled up in a chair).

When a client displays incongruent behavior, there usually are reasons for the incongruity. Understanding the reasons why clients present themselves differently from the way in which they feel is crucial to the development of a diagnostic plan.

When practitioners *stop, look,* and *learn* about their clients, they gather important information that may be relevant to the development of a diagnostic plan. The relevancy as well as the accuracy of observational inferences will be supported (or contradicted) during the ongoing interactions between the psychiatrically disabled client and the reha-

Table 6.
Inferences and the Related Observations

Category	Diagnostic Inference	Observations of Behavior and/or Appearance
Energy Level	Low	Slumped in chair
		Poor muscle tone
		Slack facial muscles
Feeling(s)	Down	Slack facial expression
		Slouched posture
Skill(s)	Adequate grooming skills	Clean, neat appearance
	Inadequate fitness	Poor muscle tone
	Inadequate attending	Not facing squarely, slumped
		in chair, no eye contact
		eyes looking at floor

bilitation practitioner. Skillful and purposive observation merely ensures that the practitioner makes comprehensive use of the nonverbal cues that the client is continually providing.

Practice Situations

Observing the client below, what can you tentatively infer about her energy level, feelings, and skills? Using a format similar to Table 7, list your initial inferences and the observations that suggest the inferences.

In making observations about energy level, the practitioner may ask and answer the following question: "What does this feature of the client's behavior or appearance tell me about his or her energy level?" Four specific areas on which to concentrate in making observations about energy level are *body build, posture, grooming,* and *nonver-*

Table 7.

Practice Format for Inferences and the Related Observations

Category	Diagnostic Inference	Observations of Behavior and/or Appearance
Energy Level	_____	_____
	_____	_____
	_____	_____
Feeling(s)	_____	_____
	_____	_____
	_____	_____
Skill(s)	_____	_____
	_____	_____

bal expressions. Observations in each area can be tied to specific and objectively verifiable visual cues (e.g., "she's five-foot-five, about one-hundred-sixty pounds" as opposed to "she's too heavy"; "he wears clean, tailored clothes" as opposed to "he's a sharp dresser").

Now think about a client or other person you know. Picture how she or he looked during your last interaction. What can you say about that person's energy level, feelings, and skills? Using a format similar to Table 7, list your initial inferences and the observations that suggest the inferences.

Finally, as you interact with your clients, begin to observe their body build, posture, grooming, nonverbal expression, and possessions. Practice formulating inferences relative to energy level, feelings, and skills. For the next few weeks, you might keep a log of your diagnostic inferences. This will help both to build your repertoire of observations and to check out your earlier diagnoses based on the ongoing interaction.

OBSERVING NONVERBAL BEHAVIOR AND APPEARANCE: A SUMMARY

Goal: To be able to make diagnostic inferences about the client based on observable data.

1. Attend to the client.
2. Observe the client's nonverbal behavior and appearance (e.g., body build, posture, grooming, and nonverbal expressions).
3. Make inferences about the client's energy level and feelings based on these observations.
4. Observe also the client's nonverbal behaviors and appearance outside of the treatment-interview setting.
5. Make inferences about the client's skill behaviors based on these observations.

LISTENING FOR VERBAL CUES

Another way in which the practitioner can gather important data concerning a client's condition is by listening. Just as the practitioner's observing skills are in part a function of his or her attending skills, a practitioner's listening skills are related to the skillfulness with which she or he both attends and observes. Observing can be conceived of as a type of "visual listening." Interestingly, a person who conveys that she or he is visually listening (observing) will increase the *verbal* output of the speaker (Mehrabian, 1972). Additional research findings suggest that it is the listener's combined use of both observing and listening skills that allows identification of discrepancies and incongruities between the speaker's verbal and nonverbal behaviors.

Common sense tells us that, because we have spent so much of our time in listening situations, we should be very good at it. Unfortunately, communication research suggests that immediately after listening to a short talk, a person remembers only one-half of what he or she has heard. This is not because the listener has not had time to listen. Most people are capable of comprehending speech at a rate three to four times faster than normal conversation. Thus, most listeners have plenty of time to think. The key to effective listening appears to be how a listener uses the extra "thinking time." An in-depth analysis of the skill of listening, as well as a review of some of the early research into listening, can be found in Barker (1971).

Basically, the skill of listening involves the practitioner's ability to hear and recall all the important verbal cues that have been presented by the client. As in observing, the practitioner will want to listen for cues that reflect the client's energy level, feeling, and skills. In addition, the practitioner will want to listen for the specifics of the situation (i.e., the who, what, when, where, why, and how).

It is important to note that there are certain types of messages that are easier to listen to than others. For example, the beginning and end of a phrase; an organized story with a beginning, middle, and end; an experience common to the listener — these are all types of content to which it is easier to listen. Unfortunately, psychiatrically disabled clients do not often talk in a sequential manner nor are their experiences necessarily common to the rehabilitation practitioner. Thus, it becomes even more important for the practitioner to be a skilled listener.

There are two basic areas of focus in listening. These are the *content* of the client's expression and the *tone of voice* used in formulating the expression. In terms of content, the practitioner listens for the actual words that give cues to client energy level, feelings, skills, and the specifics of what is happening in the client's life. In terms of voice tone, the practitioner listens to the volume (loudness or softness) and the rate or rapidity of the client's speech for cues to energy level and feelings. Noticeable *changes* in voice tone are especially important cues to a client's energy level and feeling state.

In diagnosing *energy level,* rate of speech and volume are both critical. In addition, content that reflects involvement in many activities and/or taking the initiative in a situation indicates high energy. Slow speech and content that indicates such things as having difficulty getting started at tasks suggest low energy.

Content can also be used to diagnose *feelings*. The practitioner can listen to determine if the client is actually using a feeling word (good, bad, angry, scared, etc.) to describe his or her reaction to the situation. Often, however, the client will not use a specific feeling word. In these cases, the practitioner will want to listen to the tone of voice for the verbal cues to the feeling. At a minimum, the practitioner can ask him or herself if the client is reacting with a positive, negative, or neutral feeling. A more detailed analysis of feeling could involve the practitioner listening to the client's content and asking, "If I were the client in this situation, how would I feel?"

Making diagnostic inferences about the client's *skills* involves primarily the verbal content. The client's comments about interests, values, past accomplishments, and present activities all imply the presence or absence of specific client skills. For example, a client who says, "I never finished high school because I spent so much time working on my car and joyriding with the guys," may have provided some information about his study skills, friendship skills, driving skills, and mechanical skills.

In short, then, the practitioner will want to be able to summarize accurately the important elements of the client's statement (i.e., those elements that relate to the client's energy, feeling, skills, and unique situation). As an example, consider the following client statement: "Gee, my older brother is such a pain! He really makes me mad. He's always telling me I should do stuff the way he did it. He never lets me do it my way!" From this statement, the practitioner may ask and answer the question, "What did I hear in terms of energy level, feeling, skills, and the unique situation?" The answer to this question might yield the inferences presented in Table 8.

The procedures outlined above may seem very complex for simply listening to a client — but they are the key to really coming to understand the client. The practitioner who wants to be an effective listener can engage in four steps. First, the practitioner will want to *suspend his/her own judgment.* This means letting the words sink in rather than simply judging what is being said (e.g., "That's really healthy."; or, "This person is just denying everything."). The second step is to *resist distractions.* A good attending posture helps because it facilitates focusing on the client. The practitioner can check him or herself out by determining whether he or she is thinking only about the client or is letting irrelevancies intrude (e.g., looking at the view, thinking about being hungry or about all the work that still needs to be done). The third step is to *pick out key words or phrases.* Key words and phrases are those that identify a client's energy, feelings, skills, and unique situation. The fourth and final step is to reflect on the *content and tone* as to the implications for energy, feelings, and skills.

Important information about energy and feelings can also be gathered from listening for the degree of client congruence. Discrepancies between voice tone, verbal content, and/or between nonverbal and verbal expressions can all indicate areas of conflict for the client. For example, a slumped posture, a slow, low voice tone, and the statement, "I am so happy at my job," indicate an area of client incongruency. The inference for energy might be that the client has a moderate-to-low energy level because of a conflict between how "low" he or she feels (posture) and how high (content) he or she imagines he or she should be feel-

Table 8.
Inferences and the Related Content and/or Tone

Category	Diagnostic Inference	Content and/or Tone
Energy Level	High	Intensity of voice tone (suggested by exclamation points). Use of word "always" and "never" — client may keep trying.
Feeling(s)	Mad	Used the word "mad."
Skill(s)	Inadequate assertive skills	"Never lets me do it my way."
Situation		
Who	Client and older brother	Stated content
What	Not let him do things own way	Stated content
When	Always	Stated content
Where	No data	
Why	No data	
How	No data	

ing. In the area of skills, a client's content description of a skilled behavior might conflict with the tone of voice: "I've played the piano for fifteen years. It gave me much pleasure. I even did concert tours." Said in a low tone of voice, the incongruence between the content and the tone of voice can lead the practitioner to consider the inference that the client feels, in general terms, "mixed up" or "torn" about her musical skills.

Practice Situations

As a starting point, read the client statement below. Based on this statement, develop a diagnosis of the energy level, feelings, skills, and unique situation of the client.

"Those damn bosses down there never make clear what they want! Every time there's a new job to do, they give some general direction and then yell at you when it goes wrong! I want to do a good job. Maybe it's me...I don't know."

Now think about an interaction you have had with a client or friend. Take one particular topic that you explored with that person and develop a diagnostic summary of the client in relation to the particular topic explored. Use a format similar to Table 9.

For each of the clients you work with, practice listening to what they say. At the end of each interview, develop a summary of the diagnostic inferences you have made of the client in relation to each of the situations explored during the interview. This task will serve as a valid check for you as to how well you were actually using your listening skills and in what areas you might need improvement.

Summarily, with respect to the three interrelated skills of attending, observing, and listening, the research literature, common sense, and observations of clinical practice all seem to suggest that these three major skills are both causative and cumulative skills. First of all, these skills are cumulative in the sense that the practitioner can improve his or her observing skills by carefully attending; similarly, a practitioner can improve his or her listening skills by observing and attending well. However, not only are these three skills cumulative in terms of the practitioner's performance, but they are also causative in terms of their effects on the client. The successive implementation of each of these skills helps to bring about the desired behavior in the client, which, in turn, allows for the more successful use of the practitioner's other diagnostic skills. Thus, the client who appears for help becomes the subject of the practitioner's constant attending skills, which, in turn, facilitate the client's expression of nonverbal behavior. The client, while ex-

Table 9.
Practice Format for Inferences and the Related Content and/or Tone

Category	Diagnostic Inference	Content and/or Tone
Energy Level		
Feeling(s)		
Skill(s)		
Situation		
Who		
What		
When		
Where		
Why		
How		

pressing her or himself nonverbally, becomes the subject of the practitioner's observing skills, which, in turn, facilitate the client's verbal expressions. The verbal expressions of the client then become the target of the practitioner's listening skills. It is this combination of the practitioner's attending, observing, and listening skills that facilitates the client's expression of personally relevant material to which the practitioner may skillfully *respond* — a skill that is the subject of the next section.

LISTENING FOR VERBAL CUES: A SUMMARY

Goal: To be able to make diagnostic inferences about the client based on verbal data.

1. Attend and observe the client.
2. Resist distractions.
3. Suspend own judgment about what is being said.
4. Listen to voice tone (volume, rate of speech, changes in tone) for cues as to energy level and feelings.
5. Listen and be able to summarize the content that relates to energy level, feelings, skills, and the client's unique situation.
6. Make inferences from the content and voice tone about energy level, feelings, skills, and the client's unique situation.

RESPONDING TO THE CLIENT'S VERBAL AND NONVERBAL EXPRESSIONS

Attending, observing, and listening skills are basically nonverbal skills. At the same time these skills are being used, a rehabilitation practitioner obviously needs to make skilled verbal responses in order to facilitate the client's exploration of his or her unique rehabilitation situation. The accuracy of these verbal responses, however, is directly related to the skillfulness with which the practitioner is attending, observing, and listening. Thus, these three nonverbal skills are skills the practitioner must employ habitually; for without expert attending, observing, and listening, the practitioner's verbal responses will not facilitate meaningful client self-exploration.

The skill of responding involves the practitioner's ability to communicate to the client the extent to which the practitioner understands the client's own unique situation and feelings *as the client has presented them.* In other words, the practitioner's verbal responses show the client that he or she is really being listened to and understood. The goal of this initial phase of the diagnostic planning process, remember, is to get the client to explore the rehabilitation situation with a minimum of intrusion from the practitioner's own biases and judgments. In contrast, many psychiatrically disabled clients may have discussed their life plans in situations in which they were quizzed, judged, and/or given premature advice. The purpose of the initial phase of the diagnostic planning process is to provide psychiatrically disabled clients a different and more constructive experience — a situation in which they feel understood *from their own unique frame of reference.*

There are a number of advantages to beginning the diagnostic planning process in a purely responsive mode. No doubt the most persuasive reason is that accurate responses to a client facilitate exploration. It is the client's own discussion of her or his unique situation that provides a major input to the rehabilitation diagnostic plan and the eventual rehabilitation intervention. Indeed, most major theoretical orientations to psychiatric treatment have recognized the importance of the patient talking about what is troubling him or her. For example, Freud popularized a "talking cure" for emotional problems. Carl Rogers stressed the necessity of client self-exploration. And behaviorists routinely emphasize the importance of self-report data in behavioral assessment and treatment. In addition to these theoretical emphases, a great deal of research evidence has been amassed that indicates a significant positive relationship between the degree of client self-exploration and treatment outcome. That is, those clients who talk in greater detail about their unique problems and situations are more apt to improve over the course of helping. A summary of some of the early research on the self-exploration dimension can be found in Truax and Carkhuff (1967).

One reason for the increasing number of studies on client self-exploration has been the development of reliable and observable rating scales by means of which the dimension of self-exploration can be analyzed. The most widely used scale of self-exploration, upon which countless numbers of research investigations have been carried out, can be found in Carkhuff (1969). A variation of that self-exploration scale is used in this text.

One of the most significant scientific discoveries in treatment research has been the finding that the client's self-exploration can be directly influenced by the practitioner's responding skills. These practitioner skills, once referred to as the facilitative conditions of empathy, respect, and genuineness, are now operationalized in the practitioner skill of responding. A series of experimental studies has found that a practitioner can deliberately increase and decrease a client's depth of self-exploration by directly changing the level of his or her own responses. The research results showed that when the practitioners were most responsive, the client's self-exploration was much more personally relevant; when these same practitioners became less responsive, the client's exploration became less personal. In addition, the effects on client self-exploration of relatively unskilled practitioners was also studied. These investigations discovered that the practitioner who is unskilled in responding will, over time, decrease the client's level of self-exploration.

This is not to say that the client has no role to play in how willing he or she is to explore personally relevant material. Some clients are certainly more willing to explore themselves than are others. However, the research supports the belief that irrespective of the client's own ability and willingness to explore, the responding skills of the practitioner can directly influence client self-exploration and that the clients who have practitioners unskilled in responding will gradually introduce less and less personally relevant material into the helping interaction. The pioneering research studies that investigated the relationship between practitioner responsive skills and helped self-exploration are Cannon and Pierce (1968); Holder, Carkhuff, and Berenson (1967); Piaget, Berenson, and Carkhuff (1967); and Truax and Carkhuff (1965).

The skills of responding are also important in that they can help the practitioner to build rapport with the client and to develop a meaningful practitioner-client relationship. The impression fostered in the client is that the practitioner can indeed understand him or her. If this type of relationship is established, the client will have more confidence in what the practitioner says and does. In other words, the practitioner will become a more potent reinforcer in the client's world and, in later stages of the rehabilitation process, can serve as a positive influence for the client who is working toward rehabilitation goals.

Along these lines, several experimental studies have demonstrated that responding skills can affect the outcome of a verbal conditioning or verbal reinforcement program. The effectiveness of a conditioning or a reinforcement program was found to be, in part, a function of the level of responding skills exhibited by the experimenter/helper. Two research studies that have found this relationship are Mickelson and Stevic (1971) and Vitalo (1970).

The most significant and meaningful finding with respect to the relationship between responding skills and program outcome has undoubtedly been made not in the field of psychiatric treatment *per se* but in the field of education. Over the past decade, one finding has consistently emerged from educational research: A positive relationship exists between the teacher's responding skills and various measures of student achievement and educational outcome. Thus, a teacher's ability to respond to her or his students will affect how much the students learn. More recent studies have shown that the teacher's responding skills are not only positively related to educational outcome criteria but also to criteria that have been primarily the goals of guidance counselors and other mental health professionals — goals like improved student self-concept and decreased student absenteeism. A recent summary of these studies concerned with the relationship between the teacher's responding skills and student outcome can be found in Aspy and Roebuck (1978).

In summary, then, rehabilitation practitioners have much to gain by using responding skills. First, the use of such skills will directly influence the amount of personally relevant material the clients will express to the practitioners. Second, when it comes time for the practitioners to implement treatment programs for their clients, the practitioners can improve the outcomes of these client programs if they are able to respond skillfully to the clients' experiences.

There are essentially four different types of responding skills, each of which is capable of demonstrating an understanding of the client so as to encourage the client's further exploration. These four types of responding skills are *responding to content, responding to feeling, responding to feeling and content*, and *responding with questions*.

RESPONDING TO CONTENT

Responding to content involves communicating an accurate understanding of the unique situation *as it is presented by the client.* In other words, a response to content seeks to accurately summarize the unique situation of the client. A good response to content includes any information about who, what, when, where, why, and how expressed by the client. It can also reflect any incongruities *explicitly* stated by the client. The response should be as brief as possible. That is, rambling or nonessential elements detract from a good response. Such communication helps to ensure that the practitioner's understanding will be heard by the client. Finally, a good response to content is stated in the practitioner's own words. It does not simply "parrot" back the content expressed by the client. Rather, the response rephrases the client's original expression in a fresh way. Formats that can be used to respond to content include, *"You're saying _____,"* or *"In other words _____."* A good response to content does not imply that the practitioner agrees with all that the client says. It simply means that she or he accurately understands the situation as the client sees it.

As an example, consider the following client statement:

"I really don't know what to do. My parents have been pushing secretarial training for a long time and that's what I thought I wanted, too. But now I'm taking a typing course and I don't like it."

A content response to this client might be, *"So you're saying you don't know whether or not secretarial training is right for you."*

Practice Situations

Look at the client statement concerning problems with the boss that you worked with earlier. Formulate a response to the client based on that earlier expression.

Here are three other client statements to which you can practice formulating responses to content.

     Client I: (Thirty-one-year-old hospitalized male)
                    "I'm just so tired all the time. I don't know if it's the medication or what. I just don't want to get up in the morning. I go through the day like a robot."

     Client II: (Forty-five-year-old female outpatient)
                    "Things are really looking better than they have in a long time. I really like my job and feel that I'm getting along well with the people."

     Client III: (Nineteen-year-old female outpatient)
                    "That family of mine — they're ridiculous! They're so embarrassed by my coming home. I'm the one with the problem. You'd think they'd be glad I want some help. I feel like telling them to just get lost!"

Continue to practice by making content responses to your clients. By employing responses to content in the early phases of the diagnostic interview, you will not only be facilitating client self-exploration but you will also be checking out whether you are capable of understanding the client. In addition, your responding-to-content skills will allow the client to ascertain whether you really are capable of understanding him or her.

RESPONDING TO FEELING

The goal of this particular skill is to aid clients in identifying and expressing their feelings about themselves and the situations in which they find themselves. This is not always an easy task for clients. There are a number of reasons for this. Some clients are simply not aware of their real feelings. Others think that their feelings are irrelevant and the only thing that matters is the facts. Still other clients believe that it is a sign of weakness to express feelings to anyone besides a few friends. The psychiatrically disabled client has often come to ignore his or her affective world since the feelings have either been ignored by others or have been denied *("You shouldn't get angry at Harold. He has problems of his own."; "Don't feel bad — things will work out in the end.")* For all these reasons, the practitioner must frequently and deliberately identify the client's feelings so that the client can explore these feelings; in this way, the client's emotional reaction as well as the situational facts become part of the diagnostic information.

At the opposite extreme are those psychiatrically disabled clients who have become "lost" in their feelings. Such clients are constantly overwhelmed by a multitude of feelings. In this case, the rehabilitation practitioner might have to identify the most dominant feeling and then try to respond by linking the feelings to specific content or even by just responding only to the content.

The skill of responding to feeling involves the ability to capture in words the specific feeling experience presented by a client. In this way, the practitioner facilitates the client's exploration by accurately labeling the feelings presented by the client. Explicit labeling gives the client a chance to check the practitioner out and see that she or he is an understanding person with whom it is constructive to explore.

In order to respond to feeling most effectively, the practitioner will first want to *position* him or herself for attending. This will enable him or her to see and hear clearly. Second, the practitioner will want to *observe,* focusing particularly on those cues of body build, posture, grooming, and nonverbal expression that are indicative of the client's feelings. Third, the practitioner will want to *listen* to the content and tone of the client's presentation. Again, he or she must focus on the words that indicate the client's feelings. Fourth, the practitioner will want to *summarize* what has been seen and heard that is indicative of feeling. Fifth, the practitioner identifies the *specific feeling, word, or phrase* that best reflects the client's own feeling. To do this, the practitioner can ask her or himself, "If I were the client and was saying and doing these things, how would I feel?" Identify a general feeling category first (happy, angry, sad, confused, scared, strong, or weak), pinpoint the intensity of the feeling (high, medium, or low), and then select a word or phrase that reflects this feeling area and level of intensity. Sixth, the practitioner can *check out the chosen feeling expression* to see if it is appropriate for the client. (For example, it would not be appropriate to use the word "morose" to capture the gloomy experience of a client with a sixth-grade level of education). Seventh and finally, the practitioner may *communicate the expressed feeling* using a simple, straightforward format such as, "You feel _____," or "That's a _____ feeling."

It must be emphasized that the initial task is to respond in a way that is interchangeable with the feelings expressed by the client. The aim, therefore, is to express the same feeling as that expressed by the client — no more, no less. Clients exhibit many moods that must be responded to during the diagnostic interview. Some feelings that often dominate clients are those that involve sadness and weakness. But at times clients experience "up" moments. It is critical to be able to respond to these feelings, also. Ultimately, the client must move to overcome weaknesses and utilize assets. This cannot happen unless good moments can also be shared by the practitioner.

By the same token, the psychiatrically disabled client may be struggling to express some very strong feelings of anger. Practitioners are frequently hesitant about responding to these feelings. It is as if they believe that, if they respond to these feelings openly, the client will do something disastrous. In fact, the opposite is true. If the practitioner responds, the likelihood is increased that the client will explore the feeling and come to understand it rationally. If hateful feelings are not explored, the client may well not learn to deal with them and thus may be more likely to engage in destructive actions.

Practice Situations

In order to prepare to respond fully and accurately to the feelings of clients, it is necessary to have a rich "feeling vocabulary." Experience has indicated that most practitioners dealing with psychiatrically disabled clients have inadequate feeling vocabularies for accurately capturing the client's experience. Therefore, as an initial step, it is necessary to develop an enlarged feeling vocabulary. The vocabulary can include actual feeling words such as "mad" or "annoyed" or feeling phrases such as "see red" or "punch in the nose" that capture a particular mood. Using the matrix in Table 10 to guide you, try to develop five to ten words in each category.

Once you have developed a feeling vocabulary, you can start to practice your responding. As an example, let us once again return to the client who was saying that she was unsure about wanting to pursue secretarial training. After going through the steps outlined earlier, you might respond, *"You feel confused."*

Next, formulate a response to the client whose problem involved the directions received on the job. Be sure to really think through the response, using all the steps.

As a second example, read the statement below and formulate a response to feeling.

The client is a thirty-eight-year-old female at an outpatient clinic. During the first interview she makes the statement below:
"I don't know. I just can't sleep nights. I lie awake with a million things running through my mind. Some of the things are little — like thinking about the chores I have to do around the house. But some are pretty big. Like, am I really getting the things I should out of my life?"

Now return to the three earlier client expressions to which you have already formulated content responses. This time, however, formulate a response to the feeling expressed in each of these statements.

You can continue to practice responding to feeling with clients and other people whom you want to explore things with you. As you practice, the seven steps involved in responding to feeling should become routine. Be sure to note whether or not your responses encourage your clients to talk more about their feelings.

Table 10.
Feeling Categories

FEELING CATEGORIES

INTENSITY	Happy	Angry	Sad	Confused	Scared	Strong	Weak
Strong							
Moderate							
Weak							

RESPONDING TO FEELING AND CONTENT

Feelings are about content; that is, we feel a certain way because of certain experiences we have had. When we combine the response to feeling with a response to content, we are putting the feeling together with the reason for it. This helps to clarify the basis for the feelings for both the practitioner and the client. It facilitates the client exploring both areas — feelings and content.

As shown previously, it is possible to respond separately to content and to feeling. Responding to feeling and content together simply combines both steps. Formats to use are simple ones like, *"You feel ___(feeling)___ because ___(content)___;"* or, *"That's a ___(feeling)___ feeling when ___(content)___;"* or, *" ___(content)___ can make you feel ___(feeling)___."*

For example, the combined response to the client unsure about secretarial training might be, *"You feel confused because your parents want you to take up secretarial training and you aren't sure if it's what you want."*

Practice Situations

Try formulating a complete response to the preceding example of the client who had a job problem.

Now use the same format to work with the woman who was experiencing sleeping difficulty.

Next, formulate combined feeling and content responses to the three clients for whom you previously formulated separate feeling and content responses.

As before, you should continue to develop your complete responding skills by integrating them into your sessions with your clients. Be sure to note if your *accurate* responses lead to more client exploration of a topic.

The basic task in developing responses is to formulate complete responses (i.e., to both feeling and content). This does not mean that responses to content alone or feeling alone are inappropriate. If the client is wary of expressing feelings, for example, it may be best to only respond to content in the initial phases. On the other hand, a client may give you enough cues to understand the feeling but not enough to let you know the reason. In this case, it would be appropriate to just respond to the feeling.

In summary, responses to content will generally assist the client in exploring content. Responses to feeling will elicit exploration of feeling. Responses to both feeling and content will elicit exploration in both areas — and the relationship between feeling and content will be clearer. Depending upon the particular goal of the moment and the needs of the client, any one of the three types of responses could be appropriate. The one constant among all these responses is that they are all *interchangeable* with various parts of the client's comments. That is, they mirror the client's exploration from his or her own frame of reference rather than add to or interpret the client's remarks from the practitioner's point of view.

RESPONDING WITH QUESTIONS

One other skill is required to facilitate the client's exploration of his or her situation: *question-asking*. The skill of questioning allows the practitioner to develop more detailed knowledge of the client's experience because it serves to point the client toward a specific area of exploration.

It will be recalled from the overview presented earlier that during this diagnostic phase the client needs to explore in detail his or her unique situation and feelings about that situation. The client will invariably present enough verbal or nonverbal cues for the practitioner to begin the diagnostic interview by merely responding to the client's expressions. This will ensure that the client's first attempt at describing his or her situation will come from the client's own perceptions of that situation.

In general, responding to content and feelings is preferable to responding with questions. The reasons are several:

a. Questions communicate a *lack* of understanding at a time when the practitioner's goal is to communicate an ability to understand.

b. Frequent questions may imply to the client that the practitioner is the problem solver. This may induce the client to become a passive recipient rather than an active and responsible participant in the diagnostic process. The false expectancy may be that the practitioner has the solution as long as the client answers the questions.

c. Questions introduce an element of judgment about what is and is not important in the diagnostic planning process. Questions may subtly discourage the client from divulging information that the client feels is important because the practitioner seems to be interested in other information.

d. Questions may be perceived by the client as probing and put the client on the defensive, thus hindering the development of trust and respect that responding skills create.

e. Questions about feelings are rarely appropriate. A practitioner who has been attending, observing, and listening should be able to check out a client's feeling with a response — not a question. The need to ask a client what he or she is feeling usually indicates that the practitioner has not been observing and listening. Question-asking is typically directed at the content of the client's self-exploration.

47

However, there are times when responding needs to be supplemented by skillful question-asking. Question-asking is particularly useful when the practitioner's responding can no longer sustain the client's self-exploration; or when the client's self-exploration has become less and less personally relevant; or when a piece of information that the practitioner deems potentially important has not been disclosed voluntarily by the client.

By implication, then, most of the questions the practitioner will ask during the exploration phase of diagnostic planning will relate to the unique situation of the client. The general strategy for asking questions is the 5WH strategy (who, what, why, when, where, how) suggested earlier in the section on listening. More specifically, the practitioner will want to know things such as:

Who is (was) involved?

What are (were) they doing?

Where does (did) this happen?

When does (did) this happen?

Why does (did) this happen?

How did the incident end?

The above are obviously examples of *types* of questions that the practitioner can develop using a 5WH strategy. Many practitioners may wish to use variants of these basic interrogatives. For example, the question *"Can you describe it in more detail?"* is really a *"What were they doing?"* variation. The major point is that these six basic interrogatives can be used to comprehensively cover the details in a particular situation.

Three more points are relevant to question-asking. First, the questions need to relate as closely as possible to the topic being discussed. Second, questions need to be framed to invite exploration rather than a simple yes or no response from the client. Third, any question that is worth asking is worth responding to. Thus, questions will be preceded and followed by responses to content and/or feeling. In this way, the diagnostic interviewing process will be more coherent and understandable to the client. Questions should not just appear out of thin air. The diagnostic process is often difficult and confusing enough without the interjection of mysterious questions. The idea is not to spring questions on the client but, rather, to let him or her experience how they relate to the previous material. The following is an example of a question preceded and followed by responses:

Client: *"I really don't know what to do. My parents have been pushing secretarial training for a long time and that's what I thought I wanted, too. But now I'm taking a typing course and I don't like it."*

Practitioner:	"You feel confused because your parents want you to enter a secretarial training program and you aren't sure if it's what you want."
Client:	"I guess I am wondering if I would like being a secretary."
Practitioner:	"You feel worried because you want to choose a career that you'll like. Have you looked into learning more about other careers?"
Client:	"Ever since I was a little kid, I thought I'd like to be a secretary so I never looked into anything else. I don't think I'd know how to look into something new."
Practitioner:	"You feel uncertain about how to go about exploring other careers."

Practice Situations

You have already responded to the client having difficulty with problems at work. Now formulate a question for that same client.

Try formulating questions to put to the other clients to whom you have already practiced responding in this chapter.

As you interact with your own clients, begin integrating questions where they are needed. When possible, be sure that you respond instead of asking questions. Be sure also that your questions are followed by responses to the client's subsequent answers. Questions are especially useful in opening up areas of investigation that the client has avoided. The client and practitioner often have a "set" to discuss a specific environmental area (i.e., either the client's living, learning, or working environment). This "exclusive" set is often a function of the rehabilitation referral (i.e., the client is usually referred because of problems or potential problems in the home, school, or work environments). However, it may also be important for the practitioner to check out the client's functioning in the other areas as well. For example:

"Mr. Jones, you have been talking about some things related to your desire to return to school. You haven't mentioned your family's thoughts about this and I'm wondering what they think about your desires for further schooling?"

In the above question about the as-yet-undiscussed living environment, the practitioner initially responded in the first sentence with a summary description of the preceding interview content and then asked a "what" question with respect to what the family might be thinking.

Another question that often needs to be asked at some point deals with the specific content that makes a client feel good or bad (depending upon what the client has heretofore been emphasizing). Clients are referred to rehabilitation practitioners because they have problems or deficits that need to be overcome. However, clients also have strengths and it is just as important to get the client to disclose what these strengths are. For example:

> *"Mrs. Hart, you've talked rather disgustedly about how you disliked your last job. I'm wondering, because you did work at it for one year, if there was anything you enjoyed about it?"*

This time, the question was preceded by a summary response to the client's expressed feelings and content.

The response to the client's answer would then be framed to encourage the client to explore this unknown feeling-and-content area.

RESPOND TO CLIENT'S VERBAL AND NONVERBAL EXPRESSIONS: A SUMMARY

Goal: To facilitate the client's exploration of his or her own unique situation.

1. Attend, observe, and listen to the client.

2. Respond to *content* by communicating to the client a rephrasing of the client's expression.

3. Respond to *feeling* by:
   a. summarizing the content indicative of feeling;
   b. identifying the general feeling-category;
   c. identifying the feeling intensity; and
   d. communicating an appropriate feeling word or phrase; or

4. Respond to *feeling and content* by:
   a. formulating both a content and a feeling response;
   b. combining them in a format that identifies the feeling and the content as the reason for the feeling; and
   c. communicating the feeling and content to the client; or

5. Respond with *questions* by:
   a. responding first with feeling and/or content;
   b. identifying a need for certain information;
   c. asking the 5WH type of questions to obtain this information; and
   d. responding with feeling and/or content to the client's answer.

SPECIFYING THE CLIENT'S SITUATIONAL PROBLEM(S) AND REHABILITATION GOAL(S)

The major purpose of promoting the client's self-exploration is to obtain information about the client's presenting problems and potential goals. Although much of the information obtained during this self-exploration may also prove useful during the later phases of the diagnostic planning process, the information is of immediate value in specifying the client's situational problem(s) and rehabilitation goal(s).

Rehabilitation client's are usually referred to the rehabilitation practitioner because of some obvious situational problem. Some examples of these problems were given in the first chapter and include such difficulties as the lack of a job, school failure, social isolation, and/or no place to live. However, the rehabilitation practitioner must be cautious in accepting the referral problem as the "true" problem or as the only problem. Even clients who are self-referred may not be able to accurately articulate their major problems. For example, a client or the referral source may indicate that a client's problem is that she does not have a job. Upon exploration of the client's situation, the rehabilitation practitioner may discover that another of the client's problems is that she does not have a realistic job-goal. This type of more detailed and accurate information about the client's problem will only be uncovered if the practitioner takes the time to skillfully respond to the client's feelings and content, and question the client about her unique situation.

The term *situational problem* is used deliberately. In rehabilitation, all problems must be specified with reference to the client's functioning in a certain situation. The problem is never identified as "existential anxiety" or "delusional behavior" or "extreme depression." Rehabilitation is a process whose goal is to affect the client's functioning within a certain community or environment. Thus, the situational problem is always specified with respect to a *certain environment* of people or places. Thus, it is not specific enough to state the client's problem as "poor interpersonal relationships." The practitioner will want to specify with whom or in what situation these "poor interpersonal relationships" are manifested. A similarly vague problem specification would be "lacks goals or direction." Such a problem as this needs to be further specified as to what particular environment(s) the client exhibits this lack of goals.

During the client's self-exploration, many situational problems will be mentioned. The problems will range in significance to the client. The *intensity* of feeling expressed by the client when talking about different problems will indicate the problem's importance. Also, the number of times a problem is mentioned will vary. Problems that are *frequently* talked about by the client are obviously more important. As the client explores the various situational problems he or she is experiencing, the practitioner can list the more important problems on a piece of paper.

The list of important situational problems can be shared and reviewed with the client. The client's reactions to the problem list can stimulate further client exploration and practitioner understanding of the client's feelings about the importance of the various problems. At some point, the practitioner will want to facilitate the selection of several (1-3) of the listed problems for the immediate focus of the diagnostic planning process.

Through the process of client self-exploration, in conjunction with referral information and information from significant others (see Chapter 5 of this text), the practitioner and client will be able to select the client's specific situational problem or problems that will be the focus of the diagnostic planning process. Once the situational problem has been identified, the rehabilitation goal must then be specified. The rehabilitation goal is simply the "flip side" of the problem. Its specification serves to focus the client on what benefits will be received from overcoming the problem.

For example, the situational problem of "not being able to find competitive employment" simply becomes the goal of "being able to find competitive employment." At first glance, this step seems so simple as to not even be worth mentioning. However, it needs to be mentioned for one major reason. Some practitioners mistakenly identify a rehabilitation goal that is not the reverse of the situational problem. By committing this error, the practitioner has acted as if two problems were actually one. For example, a problem that was specified as "poor grades in school" could have its goal erroneously specified as "increasing the amount of time the client studies." Increased study-time may or may not be a factor in the poor school grades. The rehabilitation goal, however, is simply to "improve school grades." Whether or not the client's study behavior contributed to the situational problem will be identified in the understanding phase of the diagnostic planning process.

Another example of incorrect goal specification would be a client whose situational problem is "being unable to transport self to work," and whose rehabilitation goal is incorrectly stated as "teaching the client how to drive to work." Once again, improving the client's ability to drive may not be the only skill that is relevant to overcoming this situational problem; improving the client's ability to use public transportation might be another. Thus, at this phase of the diagnostic planning process, the rehabilitation goal would simply be to "enable the client to transport self to work."

Practice Situations

The skill of specifying situational problems and rehabilitation goals is a relatively easy skill. The typical difficulty is not that practitioners cannot do the skill, but rather that they neglect to take the time to deliberately specify the situational problem and goal. This omission often results in confusion during later stages of the rehabilitation process.

As a way of practicing and focusing upon this skill, make a list of the common situational problems and rehabilitation goals for clients of a specific agency or rehabilitation setting. This can be done by examining your own case files or by interviewing other practitioners. Table 11 provides a chart upon which to record this information.

In performing this exercise, reflect on whether or not the common situational problems of the agency's clients are necessarily reflective of why clients may be originally referred to the agency. For example, an agency whose mission is to enable clients to become competitively employed may find that many of their clients' situational problems are related to the clients' living situations. Or, practitioners in a residential setting may find that some of their clients' situational problems and rehabilitation goals relate to a school or work environment.

Table 11. Sample Situational Problems and Rehabilitation Goals

Situational Problem	Corresponding Rehabilitation Goal
Poor grades in school	Increase school grades
Lack of a steady job	Obtain steady job
Interfering hallucinations in the workshop	Decrease interference of hallucinations in the workshop

SPECIFYING THE CLIENT'S SITUATIONAL PROBLEMS AND REHABILITATION GOALS: A SUMMARY

Goal: To identify the rehabilitation goals for which the client's strengths and weaknesses will be diagnosed.

1. Respond to the client's verbal and nonverbal expressions.

2. List the client's most significant situational problems based on such characteristics as the intensity of the client's feelings about the problem, the referral information, and information from significant others.

3. Select one, two, or three situational problems that will be the initial focus of the diagnostic planning process.

4. For each situational problem selected, identify a corresponding rehabilitation goal.

EXPLORING THE CLIENT'S UNIQUE SITUATIONAL PROBLEMS AND REHABILITATION GOALS: A SUMMARY

The practitioner skills discussed in this chapter include *informing, encouraging, attending, observing, listening, responding, and specifying.* Practitioner expertise in these skills can enable the clients to become involved in exploring their unique rehabilitation situations. A practitioner who uses these skills can provide most clients with a unique and facilitative setting in which to explore their individual rehabilitation concerns. Although the ultimate goal of the client's self-exploration is the specification of the client's problem and goal, the process by which this goal is accomplished is equally important. The interpersonal skills of the practitioner draw the client into a relationship in which the client experiences caring and support. It is this interpersonal atmosphere that helps motivate the client to become involved in the rehabilitation process.

But what of the low-functioning client who is so nonverbal or disturbed that he or she cannot even explore his or her rehabilitation concerns? Several alternatives exist. The simplest (and most nonhelpful) would be to discontinue the rehabilitation diagnostic interview until the person becomes capable of being involved in it. Another alternative would be to conduct the diagnostic planning process by interviewing significant others in the client's life and developing the diagnostic plan solely on the basis of their input and other observations of the client. Another alternative (not necessarily mutually exclusive) would be to place the client in an undemanding environment and attempt to get her or him to engage in a more structured self-exploration process with respect to that one specific setting.

A final alternative would be to plan for a more time-consuming diagnostic planning process. Responding skills can be used to facilitate self-exploration even in severely disturbed clients. Summary types of responses to content and feeling can begin to knit together in an understandable way some of the client's fragmented thoughts and messages. Then, gradually, the responses enable the client to more realistically explore the situation and his or her feelings about it. For example:

Practitioner:	*"Mrs. Parker, you've told me how you're afraid that everyone here is out to hurt you."*
Client:	*"That's right —I used to believe in God, but I don't see how I can anymore."*
Practitioner:	*"You even feel apart from your God."*
Client:	*"Well — how religious would you be in my situation?"*
Practitioner:	*"You certainly feel justified in feeling the way you do."*
Client:	*"I should have divorced my husband before he died — he put me here."*
Practitioner:	*"You're still angry about what he did to you."*
Client:	*"His mother and him."*
Practitioner:	*"Mrs. Parker, you're telling me that you feel resentful toward your deceased relatives, your God, and the people here who are trying to help you."*
Client:	*"I just wish somehow things could be different."*

In the above interchange, the practitioner deliberately tries to respond to the client so as to build a relationship based on understanding. At the same time, the practitioner's responses attempt to tie together situations that are seemingly disparate so as to enable the client to explore her own situation more coherently.

Another occasion when the use of responding skills may have to be modified is when an abbreviated diagnostic plan must be formulated in only one session. This may be due to infringements on the practitioner's time or extensive pressures on the client. In this situation, it still makes sense to respond to the client's frame of reference before developing a diagnostic plan. Even if the practitioner can only respond for five minutes, the responding skills can still have an impact by quickly giving the practitioner a chance to establish minimal rapport and ascertain the client's initial frame of reference.

EXPLORING: A SKILLED APPROACH

"A full day, huh?"

Lee looked at Ginny and gave her secretary a weary grin. "You know it. One more client today and I'd probably be ready for some rehabilitation myself!"

It was after five and the clinic had begun to gear down after the hectic scramble of a normal day's routine. The hall outside Lee's office was almost empty. Despite her weariness, Lee felt strangely happy as she returned to her desk and began sorting out the accumulated paperwork. It felt good to put in a full day. Every one of her scheduled clients had shown up. Of course, that wasn't the case every day. But Lee could still remember what it felt like to write off several hours a day for no-shows. Things certainly were looking up.

And for good reason, too. Lee could still recall the dismay she had felt the first time she stopped to think — really think — about how her clients probably felt when they approached their first session with an unknown practitioner: alone — confused — skeptical — in some cases, even frightened. And despite her own training, her own commitment as a rehabilitation practitioner, Lee had been doing little or nothing to allay such negative feelings.

Now, thank goodness, those days were past. Now she set an initial goal with each individual client: to get that client involved in the rehabilitation process and to sustain this involvement for as many sessions as it took to deal with the client's situation. Now each person scheduled for a meeting received a notice about the meeting several days ahead of time — and not a cold, impersonal form, but a brief letter that included information about parking, office location, and so on — often with a personal note of encouragement at the bottom from Lee herself. And now each client arrived for the first meeting to find that, instead of a cool professional anchored behind a desk or a chaotic practitioner surrounded by the fallout from a hundred previous clients, the person waiting for him or her was warm, relaxed, and genuinely interested in the client's own situation.

None of this was accidental, of course. Lee had made a concerted effort to use the skills she knew were required of her. She rearranged her office to make it more conducive to effective counseling. She made sure that she faced clients squarely, that she inclined herself toward them, that she made enough eye contact to let them know she was right there with them.

"I was wrong all along about my job," she thought to herself now as she wound up her day's activities. "I thought my job was to be available for helping. But my job is to deliver skills. To make a difference in my client's lives. To give them the help they need. And I sure can't do any of that unless I first get them involved!"

Getting the client involved in rehabilitation is certainly the first step. But equally important is keeping them involved — involved so that the clients are encouraged to discuss meaningful diagnostic information. The following example clearly illustrates one practitioner's skillful attempts at maximizing client involvement.

"You didn't care too much for the hospital, huh?" George leaned forward, forearms resting on his knees, and regarded the young man slumped dejectedly in the chair facing him.

"Uh uh." Ron's voice was barely a whisper. "Oh, they got me off the drugs and that was cool. But — but — it's like they didn't give me nothin' to take their place."

George responded to the content of Ron's expression: "So you're saying it was good that they took you off your drug hang-up but they left you feeling kind of empty." As he spoke, he observed his client carefully. Close to six-feet tall, Ron looked as though he could not have weighed any more than 135 or so. Since the sessions had started, he had met George's gaze only once or twice, each time flicking his eyes away as if afraid that the contact might be more than he could handle. He looked clean enough, right down to his fingernails; yet his clothes were baggy and wrinkled as though he had slept in them for nights on end. It was not difficult for George to draw several tentative inferences concerning Ron's condition: low energy level; feelings of depression combined with apprehension concerning George himself; and some clear incongruities as reflected in the contrast between his cleanliness and his poor dress.

"Yeah..." Ron seemed to draw even further into himself. "Like, I don't even know why I get outa bed in the morning. There's nothin' I can do. At least, all the things I'd like to do are just unreal. I could never do them. Those doctors didn't really change nothin'. They just got rid of stuff, that's all." During the latter part of this exchange, Ron looked up at George —not long, but long enough for George to read the emotion that was reflected in Ron's expression. He responded to this feeling.

"You feel angry, bitter almost, because they just took away what you cared about without really changing your life for the better."

And Ron looked up again, nodding now, a faint look of surprise on his face. "Yeah, they really did a number on me," he said. "Only it was their number, not mine. I never asked them to butt in."

And George kept responding. "It really makes you mad that they could just step in and mess up your life like that. Even if drugs weren't doing you any good, it was still your life and your choice."

It was a start, George knew — just the smallest sort of beginning. But he had Ron talking now, exploring his situation and the feelings he was experiencing. That's where it all had to begin. And George knew that at this stage his job was to promote Ron's exploration — not to judge, not to criticize, and not to offer advice. Only by finding out where he really was in terms of his own life, his own unique situation, could Ron ever hope to take control of that life. And delivering that control and the understanding that it entailed was what George's work was really all about.

Chapter 3 UNDERSTANDING THE CLIENT'S PERSONAL STRENGTHS AND DEFICITS

UNDERSTANDING: AN UNSKILLED APPROACH

Ray gave Suki a big smile intended to communicate as much cheerful confidence as possible.

"Well, Suki, you feel pretty ready to face the world?"

In just a few days she would be going back home again. This had been Suki's second stay in the hospital in the last year. The first time she had left after six weeks. This time she had spent almost three months in the hospital. Ray fervently hoped that she would be able to handle the complexities of her "outside" life this time around.

"Well — I guess I'm ready. I hope so."

"I'm sure you are!" Ray tried to cover his own uncertainty with a continued show of confidence. "Let me show you what I've done."

*He opened his notebook and took out a couple of sheets of paper covered with his own spidery handwriting. "We've talked about the way that you have trouble keeping on top of all the different things that pop up every day. It seems to me that the best thing will be for you to have some way of **anticipating** problems and situations. Make sense?"*

Suki had been following him carefully. Now she nodded her agreement. "Oh, yes! If I knew about problems before they happened, I know I could do better with them!"

"Good! Well, then. I went ahead and made up a kind of list. All the things I listed are what seem to me to be your own real strengths and weaknesses — the things that are easy for you and the things you have trouble with."

"I see ..." Suki was frowning, looking less certain. But Ray plowed straight ahead.

"First, some of your strengths or assets. You're a hard worker, which is good. And you're very sensitive to the needs of other people — like being able to tell when your husband is depressed about something. That's important, too," Suki nodded. "Then there are your weak areas. For one thing, you have a hard time keeping your level of energy up. You've got to plan and stick to a healthy diet — and get some good exercise, too. And you've got to organize your time better. Each night you should make a list of all the things you have to do the next day — and then stick to it. For another thing — "

Ray's voice droned on and on, listing all the areas where he felt Suki needed to focus her attention. But Suki wasn't listening anymore. He

*was talking about big problems, little problems, in-between problems —
and all jumbled up together! It was too much for her. How could she ever
cope with everything that Ray seemed to see in her? Was this really her?
Either way, the answer had to be depressing. If Ray was wrong — if he
was just imagining all these problems — then she herself still didn't
have a clue about how to act when she went home. Yet if he was right,
the problems were overwhelming. There was no way she could ever
handle it!*

*Suki had felt the beginnings of a new confidence when she came in.
But Ray's list had destroyed this. Disorganized, haphazard, jumping
from one unrelated thing to another, the list gave Suki nothing to focus
on, nothing she could hold onto. She could only sit and try to listen, all
the while feeling herself being crushed lower... and lower... and
lower...*

The previous chapter examined those practitioner skills that facilitate clients' appearance for rehabilitation services and their increasing
involvement in a self-exploration process of their own unique situations. It culminated in an initial specification of the clients' situational
problems and rehabilitation goals. However, it is not enough for clients
merely to explore their situational problems and goals. Psychiatrically
disabled clients must go beyond this exploration and learn to *understand* their rehabilitation goals in relation to their own personal
strengths and deficits.

Up to now, the practitioner skills covered have been primarily *responsive* in nature; they have reflected ways in which the practitioner
can absorb information through attending, observing, and listening
and give it back to the client in the form of responses that mirror the
client's own state. In the understanding phase of the diagnostic planning process, however, the rehabilitation practitioner focuses on skills
that are primarily *interpretive* in nature — skills that enable the practitioner to provide each client with new and more constructive insights
about his or her functioning. In particular, the practitioner seeks to help
the client to understand the *personal meaning* of his or her situational
problem(s) and goal(s), and the *personal deficits and strengths* that are
related to those problems and goals. In the process of understanding
the personal meaning of the client's situation, the rehabilitation practitioner helps the client to identify why the situation is important. This
understanding is critical to the diagnostic plan because identical situational problems and goals may mean different things to different people. For example, one client's loss of a full-time job may mean that he
cannot experience himself as a real adult. For another client, losing a
full-time job may mean that for the first time she cannot maintain the
standard of living that her family demands. Personal meanings are
critical for the practitioner to diagnose and for the client to understand

because they supply the "emotional steam" that will help the client to become motivated to overcome the personal problems.

Understanding a client's personal strengths (and deficits) involves the rehabilitation practitioner helping the client to identify those specific skill behaviors that will help (or hinder) the client's attainment of specific rehabilitation goals. To a great extent, clients often succeed or fail in rehabilitation based on their own unique pattern of strengths and weaknesses. The practitioner and the client need to understand this pattern so that skills-training programs can be designed to overcome the client's deficits *and/or* a new environment can be arranged to accommodate the client's present strengths and deficits. In either case, the efficacy of eventual rehabilitation intervention can be maximized by an understanding of the client's specific strengths and deficits.

There are essentially four possible methods that the practitioner can use to help clients understand their personal strengths and deficits. These four methods will be discussed in this chapter. No doubt the most difficult method involves making interpretations to clients about the strengths and weaknesses of which they were previously unaware or could not acknowledge. These practitioner interpretations are based on the clients' on-going self-exploration and are designed to help the clients gain insight into their own assets and deficits with respect to their own rehabilitation goals. Another method simply involves asking the clients to suggest what particular strengths and deficits the clients think are relevant to their particular rehabilitation goals. Having had the opportunity to explore their unique situations in the first phase of the diagnostic planning process, many clients will be willing and able to suggest some of their own strong and weak points. A third method involves the practitioner suggesting some relevant strengths or weaknesses based on the practitioner's previous experience with clients who had similar rehabilitation goals, or based on test data that has been collected. A fourth method involves the practitioner obtaining suggestions from significant others as to what they think are the clients' strengths and deficits with respect to the clients' rehabilitation goals.

Both of these final two methods, practitioner suggestions and significant-other suggestions, can be shared with the clients and agreed to by the clients. The concept of "personalized" strengths and deficits means that the clients understand and agree with the suggestions that these are, in fact, their own strengths and deficits. Since the clients will ultimately be involved in carrying out the rehabilitation plan, practitioner or significant-other understanding is not enough. The clients must also understand and accept the diagnoses.

When the practitioner helps the client organize his or her strengths and deficits, a comprehensive understanding of the client's diagnosed strengths and deficits can be developed. One particularly effective organization method is to *categorize the client's strengths and deficits* so that a meaningful picture of the client's functioning emerges. Simply possessing a list of the client's personal strengths and deficits is not a sufficient basis from which to help the client understand the rehabilitation treatment plan. Rather, the rehabilitation practitioner can paint a comprehensive and understandable picture of the client by means of a two-dimensional categorization process. One category pertains to whether the client's identified strengths and deficits are primarily physical, emotional, or intellectual. The other category specifies the particular environment in which these physical, emotional, and intellectual skills are relevant. That is, the practitioner identifies the living, learning, and working environments in which those previously identified client skill characteristics are manifested. From this two-dimensional categorization process emerges a picture of the psychiatrically disabled client's unique pattern of strengths and deficits as well as the specific environmental area in which these skill behaviors are exhibited. The resulting diagnostic picture is both comprehensive in scope and comprehensible in meaning.

PERSONALIZING THE MEANING OF THE CLIENT'S EXPLORATION

Before the practitioner and client begin to deliberately focus on the client's relevant strengths and weaknesses, it is important to help the client understand the personal meaning of his or her unique situation. In developing a diagnosis of the meaning, the practitioner begins to focus on *why the situation is important to the client.* The meaning of the situation must be personalized for the client. In helping the client understand the personal implications of the situation or problem, the practitioner begins to initiate a little more understanding than the client has so far been able to achieve during the exploration phase. It should be remembered that before the practitioner can begin to diagnose the personal meaning a particular situation has for a client, the practitioner will first want to have established a responsive relationship with the client. That is, the practitioner takes the client through the exploration phase first by responding to the feeling and content presented by the client. During this exploration phase, the practitioner also attempts to understand the client more deeply, which increases the chances that the personalized meaning diagnosis will be accurate. As a rule of thumb, the practitioner will want to make a minimum of six to twelve responses to feeling and content in a particular area before she or he can even entertain making a personalized response to meaning. Often it will take much longer. The client is ready for personalized meaning when feelings and facts about the situation have been developed in detail. In short, the prerequisite steps to diagnosing personalized meaning are *attending, observing, listening, responding (to feeling, to content, with questions), and specifying* the situational problems and goals. Only at this point has the practitioner earned the right to interpret the *personalized meaning*.

In order to personalize the meaning of the client's situation, the rehabilitation practitioner will want to guide the client toward an answer to the question, *"Why is the fact that this is happening important to me?"* The practitioner can facilitate this understanding by beginning to make slightly more interpretive statements, using as a guiding format:

"You feel _____ because YOU _____."

Before analyzing the personalized meaning process in greater detail, consider the following example as an illustration of the difference between an interchangeable response to feeling and content and an interpretation of personalized meaning. Let us go back to the client unsure about pursuing secretarial training. The response to feeling and content was:

"You feel confused because your parents want you to take up secretarial training and you aren't sure if you'll like it."

The response to feeling and personalized meaning might be:

"You feel worried because you want to make the right choice on this very important decision."

Note how the interchangeable response to content and feeling differs from the personalized meaning interpretation. The focus of the response has shifted from the parent's wishes (***"your parents** want you to take up secretarial training... "*) to the personal importance of these actions ***for the client ("you** want to... "*). Although the difference in sentence construction may be subtle, the potential impact on the client is very strong. When the practitioner begins to move to a personalized meaning interpretation, he or she starts to identify the client's personal role in the issue. People talk for a reason. Even when they are talking about the weather, they are mentioning it because at some level it affects them personally, even though they may not mention its personal implications. The same general process holds true for the psychiatrically disabled client during the diagnostic planning process. The client will probably begin by exploring his or her external world, especially when talking about negative feelings. Some examples are: "employers are prejudiced"; "my spouse doesn't understand"; "people abuse me"; etc. As the client explores these external situations, the practitioner guides the client to a more personal understanding of what this means in terms of the client's own functioning.

It is important that the practitioner and client agree on the personalized meaning of the situation for the client. It is the personalized meaning response that identifies why a rehabilitation intervention is necessary. In the previous client example, rehabilitation is needed not because of the anger at the parents, but because the client feels helpless about not being her own person. Unless the client can admit to this personal responsibility, she really will not be motivated to try changing the situation. Instead, she will passively wait for someone or something to change the parents.

As a further example of personalized meaning interpretation, look at the dialogue below. The client is a forty-three-year-old male who is trying to win his battle against an extensive history of alcoholism. Because of his drinking, his work record has been less than exemplary. He has not had anything to drink in almost a year and is trying to get a job on which he can support himself.

> **Client:** *"I get mad a lot because none of the employers I go to will give me the time of day."*
>
> **Practitioner:** *"It makes you angry that they ignore you."* (Interchangeable response to feeling and content)
>
> **Client:** *"Yeah. I mean, you'd think they'd at least have the courtesy to listen!"*
>
> **Practitioner:** *"It's pretty frustrating when they don't even treat you with simple decency."* (Interchangeable response to feeling and content)
>
> **Client:** *"The worst part is knowing how old I am and how there are so many young guys I have to compete with for jobs. That's really a bad feeling, seeing how much younger they are."*
>
> **Practitioner:** *"It's really discouraging, seeing yourself in the same position as these other guys but knowing you're twenty years older."* (Interchangeable response to feeling and content)
>
> **Client:** *"I'll say! Listen, these guys can afford to be patient. But me —I just can't waste any time, that's all. I just can't."*
>
> **Practitioner:** *"You feel terribly pressured because you see more of your life slipping through your fingers."* (Personalized meaning interpretation)

Here the practitioner initially responds at an interchangeable level to feeling and content in order to gain an initial diagnosis of the client. In the final response, the practitioner initiates a diagnosis of the personal meaning the situation has for the client.

A personalized meaning response brings fresh insight to the client as to why the rehabilitation process is necessary and important to her or his well-being. It may be that some psychiatrically disabled clients will move to this level of self-exploration solely by means of the responding skills of the rehabilitation practitioner. Provided with a respectful relationship and the opportunity to hear themselves explore their situation, they may dare to initiate a discussion of their more personal role in the situation. A very few clients may even be able to start their self-exploration at a personalized meaning level. Such clients as these do not need the practitioner's personalized meaning interpretation; they will do it themselves. With such rare individuals, the rehabilitation practitioner simply needs to demonstrate his or her understanding by responding interchangeably to the client's own interpretation of personalized meaning.

Typically, however, the practitioner can guide the client in the development of real insights by using personalized meaning interpretations. It is important to recognize that such interpretations are based on the client's previous explorations *and not on any one theory of personality or psychotherapy.*

The existence of many theories of psychotherapy, with new theoretical constructs being developed every year, is perhaps the clearest indication that no one theory is capable of organizing and explaining all human behavior. The current proliferation of psychotherapeutic theories is a direct reflection of the inability of any one theory to prove itself universally correct and useful. Thus, the use of interpretive skills is not a function of what theory the practitioner espouses but, rather, of how skillful the practitioner has been in understanding each client's situation and of the practitioner's own knowledge and skills in the problem area in which the client is experiencing difficulty.

The importance of the particular theoretical base of knowledge adhered to by the practitioner has been called into question by several research studies (Anthony & Carkhuff, 1970; Carkhuff, Kratochvil, & Friel, 1968). These studies suggest that, though graduate students in the helping professions improved over training in their ability to know what a helpful response is, there was no corresponding improvement in their ability to actually make a helpful response within a counseling interaction. Thus, it may be surmised that what practitioners have learned about theory does not necessarily translate into what they *do* in an interaction with a client.

These research studies, as well as the current plethora of personality and psychotherapy theories, have a fairly straightforward implication for the development of practitioner interpretive skills. That is, it is premature to make interpretations based exclusively on any one theory of psychotherapy. It would appear that at the present state of our research and theoretical knowledge, it would be most effective to assume an eclectic theoretical stance (i.e., using any theory that is appropriate *when* it is appropriate). The "appropriateness" of the theory is a function of how well the theoretical perspective allows the practitioner to make personalized interpretations to the client — a personalized statement with which the helpee can understand and agree. The goal of this personalized interpretation is not to prove theoretical constructs or persuade the client to accept a theoretical interpretation; rather, the goal is to get the client to begin to understand the personal importance of his or her own unique rehabilitation situation. Thus, the goal of personalized meaning is dramatically different from the goal of most psychotherapeutic insight approaches. There is no attempt to interpret the meaning of the client's situation in terms of developmental factors nor to attempt massive personality reconstruction. Although developmental factors and historical personality traits may have been introduced into the exploration process by the client, the rehabilitation practitioner's emphasis in the understanding stage is on the implications of past events only in terms of why they are important *in the present and future* in terms of client capabilities and abilities. The practitioner deliberately attempts to get at the *present meaning* of the client's situation. This is *best* illustrated by the practice format of, "You *feel*," as opposed to, "You *felt*." *The rehabilitation practitioner's diagnostic interviewing skills guide the client from a victimized exploration of past events to an understanding of present meaning and future directions.*

Practice Situations

Read the consecutive client statements below. Formulate an interchangeable response to feeling and content after each of the first three client statements. Then make an interpretation as to the personal meaning for the client after the fourth client statement.

Sharon is a young woman. She is intelligent but lost. She is searching to understand herself.

Sharon's Statement 1: *"Things are not going so well for me. Not in school. Not with my boyfriend. I just seem to be floundering."*

Sharon's Statement 2: *"Sometimes I just think that if people are going to act the way they do, there's no sense in trying. Like my boyfriend. One minute everything is cool. The next minute he's raising a bunch of questions about whether we should be together."*

Sharon's Statement 3: *"I'm tired of being on trial all the time. The school keeps testing you to see if you learned the stuff — and then to be with him and have him put me on trial — it's just too much!"*

Sharon's Statement 4: *"The whole thing has got me really upset."*

Now work with the client below. Again, develop a base of interchangeable responses to feeling and content. Then introduce an interpretation of personalized meaning to the fourth client statement.

Charles is a man who has been released recently from a hospital. He has been hospitalized once before. He has been trying to get a job.

Charles's
Statement 1: *"Nobody wants to give me a job. They look at the periods of no work that I have, ask me why, and then it's all over. No chance at all."*

Charles's
Statement 2: *"I'm a veteran, served my country, and nobody cares. The whole thing stinks."*

Charles's
Statement 3: *"Listen, it's like I took my chances to protect them when I was a soldier. Now I need a break and I get nothing."*

Charles's
Statement 4: *"This job hunting is leading nowhere. If I don't get a job soon, I'm going to have to get a cheaper room and other plans I have are going to start falling apart."*

As the final step in learning the skill of interpreting personal meaning, practice formulating this type of statement for clients: *"You feel _____ because you _____ ."* Be sure to lay an adequate base by first responding to feeling and content. It may also be helpful to keep a written record of what the client presented and what you said as a personalized interpretation. If the interpretation was inaccurate, try to think of other personalized interpretations you might have made to the client.

PERSONALIZING THE MEANING: A SUMMARY

Goal: To identify the personal meaning of the client's exploration.

1. Respond with content and/or feeling to the client's exploration of his or her unique situation.

2. Identify the client's role in the situation; that is, why the situation is important to the client.

3. Make a personalized meaning response using a format similar to: *"You feel _____ because you _____ ."*

PERSONALIZING THE CLIENT'S SPECIFIC STRENGTHS AND DEFICITS

In developing a diagnosis of the client's personal strengths and deficits, the practitioner helps the client focus on those specific skilled behaviors that the client *can and cannot do* that are relevant to the client's situational problem and rehabilitation goal. This attempt to identify personal strengths and weaknesses usually takes place only after the client has personalized the meaning of the situation. It is the client's acceptance of the personalized meaning of the situation that prompts the client to examine in detail his or her own specific strengths and weaknesses.

Identifying the client's strengths and weaknesses is an important step in the diagnostic process because it is the client's unique pattern of strengths and weaknesses that most affects the client's attainment of his or her rehabilitation goals. Thus, the rehabilitation diagnostician will want to identify which client strengths and deficits are specifically related to the achievement of the client's rehabilitation goals. The research that highlights the relationship between client skill performance and rehabilitation outcome has been summarized periodically — Anthony, 1979; Anthony & Margules, 1974; Anthony, Cohen, & Vitalo, 1978.

As mentioned earlier in this chapter, there are essentially four methods by which the practitioner can facilitate the client's identification of personal strengths and deficits: (1) making a personalized *interpretation* of the client's strengths and weaknesses based on the client's ongoing self-exploration; (2) obtaining the *client's suggestions* about his or her strengths and weaknesses; (3) providing the client with the *practitioner's suggestions* about the client's strengths and weaknesses, based on either the practitioner's previous experience with clients in similar situations, or based on test data; and (4) sharing with the client suggestions made by *significant others* about the client's strengths and weaknesses.

MAKING A PERSONALIZED INTERPRETATION

Similar to the process of interpreting personalized meaning, the steps to making a personalized interpretation of client's strengths and deficits are cumulative. That is, the practitioner attends, observes, listens, builds a base of responding to feeling and content, specifies the client's situational problems and goals, diagnoses the personalized meaning, and then formulates a personalized strength or deficit statement. It is primarily this base of understanding and trust developed during this first phase of the diagnostic process that facilitates the client's receptivity to the practitioner's interpretations. In order to make a personalized interpretation, the practitioner asks and then answers the question, *"What is it the client cannot do that is causing him or her difficulties?"* Or, in the case of strengths: *"What is it that the client can do that will help him or her overcome difficulties?"*

The practitioner can guide the client's understanding of his or her personal strengths and deficits by formulating the personalized interpretation in a manner similar to the following format: *"You feel _____ because you CANNOT (NEED TO) _____"*; or, in the case of a personalized strength interpretation: *"You feel _____ because you CAN _____."*

Before analyzing the process of interpreting personalized strengths and deficits in greater detail, consider the following illustration of the difference between an interchangeable response to feeling and content, a personalized meaning interpretation, and (in this case) a personalized deficit interpretation. A client who is having marital difficulties that are hampering his reintegration into his home environment makes the following statement:

Client: *"My wife just seems to want more than I can give. She says I don't appreciate her."*

Feeling and Content Response:

"You feel sad **because** your wife isn't satisfied with your relationship."*

Personalized Meaning Interpretation:

"You feel sad **because you** are not measuring up in the most important relationship of your life."*

Personalized Deficit Interpretation:

"You feel confused **because you can't** praise your wife for the things she does well and this is really hurting your relationship."*

These interpretive statements would not be made one right after the other, of course, but would be separated by periods of client self-exploration. The specific interpretations that are made are a function of that intervening client self-exploration. The above example illustrates the responses consecutively so that the distinctions between the various types of practitioner statements are more obvious. Note how the personalized deficit statement differs from the personalized meaning response in that the deficit statement specifically mentions a *behavioral skill area* in which the client is deficient. In addition, the personalized deficit interpretation is phrased in such a way as to make the client *actually responsible* for doing something about the situation. Both the personalized meaning and personalized deficit interpretations differ from the response to content and feeling in that the focus is on the *internal* and *personal* frame of reference of the client rather than on the wife's situation.

Thus, the understanding process develops from an *external exploration* of the situation to an *internal understanding* of the *client's responsibility* for actively pursuing a specific *skill behavior*. The client is guided through this exploration and understanding process by means of the responding and personalizing skills of the rehabilitation practitioner.

As indicated, it is critical that the focus be on *the client's behavior.* Consider the following response:

"You feel angry because you can't get your boss to stop criticizing you."

The specified behavior is the boss's — not the client's. If the focus of rehabilitation in this case were on changing the client's behavior, the attempt at personalized interpretation would have to be reformulated to capture the client's specific deficit. An example of such a response might be:

"You feel angry because you need to be able to really speak up and tell your boss, in an effective way, to stop criticizing you."

The second response puts the focus back on the client's specific role in the problem. When making personalized interpretations, the practitioner will want to be careful to shift the feeling word as appropriate. In other words, as the cause of the problem becomes internal rather than external, the client's feeling may well shift because the practitioner is now diagnosing feelings about self rather than about others. In the situation above, the client's feelings might well change from feeling angry at his boss to feeling disgusted with himself because he cannot tell when or how to speak up to get his boss off his back.

Practice Situations

Look at the example below. Based on the statement, practice making a personalized deficit interpretation. The first client is a woman in her mid-thirties. She has been married almost ten years and has two children. For the past couple of years, she has been working part-time.

Client 1 Statement: *"My life seems to be empty. I take pleasure in my kids, but not in either my husband or my job. I'm so bored. I've tried to look at a lot of different possibilities, but nothing looks very satisfying."*

Check to make sure that the deficit you identified as the client's deficit is a specific behavior skill area. Now read this next statement made by a male client in his late twenties. Based on the statement, practice making a personalized deficit interpretation.

Client 2 Statement: *"I'm going to kill that damn supervisor if he doesn't stop pushing me. Everything he asks is in a rude way. I'm afraid I'm really going to flip out unless something changes."*

When an appropriate responsive base has been developed, you can attempt to make personalized deficit interpretations with your clients. Remember that the goal is to get the client to agree with and understand his or her personal strengths and deficits.

PERSONALIZING STRENGTHS

Up to this point, all the examples of personalized strength and deficit interpretations have focused on deficits. However, the planning process must also diagnose the client's strengths. Personalizing client strengths is often not as difficult as personalizing deficits because people are typically much more open about what they can do well and much more defensive about what they cannot do well. Thus, the practitioner will not have to struggle to get the client to personalize strengths; rather, the client will usually come right out and tell the practitioner about his or her strengths. If these strengths are vital to the success of the rehabilitation plan, the practitioner will obviously want to verify their existence during the assessment stage of the diagnostic planning process.

There are, however, some psychiatrically disabled clients who are as reluctant to identify their strengths as they are their weaknesses. For these particular clients, the practitioner will have to make personalized interpretations of their strengths. The following example illustrates the distinction between response to feeling and content, a personalized meaning interpretation, and a personalized strength interpretation:

Client: *"The last job I had, the employment interviewer offered it to me right there on the spot. It was surprising to me."*

Feeling and Content Response:
"You're still amazed at how quickly he gave you the job."

Personalized Meaning Interpretation:
"You're pleased because you discovered you really do have some things employers are looking for."

Personalized Strength Interpretation:
"You feel confident because you can present your assets in a job interview."

In the preceding example, the practitioner identified job-interviewing skills as one strength of the client. Although the client undoubtedly has deficits (otherwise why would she or he be a candidate for rehabilitation?), it is important to recognize the client's strong points since they play a prominent role in the client's rehabilitation program. Indeed, some clients' major deficit may be an inability to place themselves in a living, learning, and/or working environment that accommodates their present strengths to the utmost. For some clients, the mere process of personalizing strengths is therapeutic in and of itself. Thus, if the client does not, the practitioner can introduce the need to identify and understand the client's personal strengths. The practitioner can introduce a discussion of strengths by responding with questions as outlined in the previous chapter.

Regardless of whether the focus is on the positive or problematic aspects of the situation, most clients must be helped to understand the personal meaning of their situations and their own unique strengths and weaknesses. Few clients can personalize their strengths and deficits without assistance from the rehabilitation practitioner.

DEFENSES AGAINST PERSONALIZING

Clients have an infinite number of strategies to defend against personal responsibilities. These strategies, quite common in the context of psychiatric rehabilitation, are methods of avoiding a personalized understanding of strengths and weaknesses. Most textbooks of abnormal psychology list common defense mechanisms (e.g., displacement, projection, rationalization, denial, etc.). In psychiatric rehabilitation, these various defense mechanisms are not seen in a psychoanalytic context but as functional behaviors, of which the client may or may not be aware, and which prevent the client from taking a personal, active responsibility for changing his or her behavior. Some examples are:

a. A client who *displaces* his anger at his boss onto his co-workers and then ends up getting fired for failure to get along with his co-workers.

b. A client who *projects* his own disrespect and distrust of teachers onto the teacher and then leaves school because the teachers do not communicate well with him.

c. A client who, lacking the skills to find employment, *rationalizes* that the economy is too poor and thus never tries to learn how to look for a good job.

d. A hospitalized client who, fearing that she cannot raise her children, *denies* that she really wants to return home and resigns herself to a long stay in the institution.

In each of the preceding examples, the clients have managed to avoid a personalized understanding of their situation by means of their defensive strategies. Until a personalized understanding occurs, they will have little motivation to become actively involved in the rehabilitation process and work toward learning assertiveness, communication, job-seeking, and parenting skills, respectively. However, it is not enough for the practitioner simply to possess an intellectual understanding of the client's defenses. The really difficult practitioner skill involves getting the client to openly explore his or her situation (responding skills) and then guiding the client to a *personal understanding* and *acceptance* of the specific deficits that he or she had heretofore been defending against.

SUPPLEMENTARY INTERPRETIVE DIAGNOSTIC SKILLS

The responding and personalizing skills that have been focused on are usually sufficient to promote the client's exploration and understanding. However, the practitioner may need to use two additional interpretive skills to help an otherwise reluctant client to understand at a personalized level either the meaning of the situation or a particular client's strength or deficit. Similar to making a personalized interpretation, these skills are also interpretive because they go beyond a mere response to the client's expressions. These two skills are named *immediacy* and *confrontation*. Briefly, the communication of immediacy refers to interpreting what is happening in the moment between the client and practitioner. Confrontation refers to the practitioner's ability to interpret to the client discrepancies in the things she or he is saying or doing.

Immediacy

At every stage of the diagnostic interviewing process, it is critically important for the practitioner to be "right there" with each client, communicating that "attentiveness" mentioned in an earlier chapter. There are times, however, when the practitioner may want to communicate the immediacy of her or his attention and concern in a more explicit way. Such immediacy of expression serves two purposes. The client's understanding is made more real because it embraces an understanding of what is happening right then and there with the practitioner. In other words, immediacy can be a key factor in helping the client to accept the diagnostic interpretation of strengths and deficits because she or he can see the problem in the "here and now" of the interaction with the practitioner. The client also learns something about the skills of communication by being presented with a model (i.e., the practitioner) who is able to communicate fully and accurately. The skilled practitioner can formulate a diagnostic response of immediacy by asking and answering several specific questions: *"How does what this client is saying about the problem relate to what is going on between us right now?" (In other words, how do the client's words reflect upon his or her relationship with the practitioner?) "Is the client acting out his or her own part in the problem?" "Does this client perceive me (the practitioner) as doing things that he or she has described others as doing?" "How does the client feel about what I'm doing or saying right now?" "Is the client acting out a problem with another person by taking that person's part?"*

A more detailed description of immediacy can be found in Carkhuff (1969). Immediacy differs from the psychoanalytic concept of transference in two significant ways: (1) it takes the practitioner's stimulus value into consideration in interpreting the client's communication; and (2) it is not tied to any one personality theory and thus is open to more broad expressions of the client's experience.

The skilled helper can make an interpretation of immediacy by using some variation of the basic format, *"Right now with me, you feel _____ because you _____."* For example, one client might express her understanding of a personalized diagnosis by saying, *"I feel pretty lonely because I can't seem to talk enough to other people to get them to like me."* At the same time, this client might be slumped down in her seat, looking away from the practitioner with the corner of her mouth turned down in a mournful expression. Making an immediacy interpretation, the practitioner might say, *"I can see that. Even here with me, you feel pretty miserable because you don't think I want to be your friend."* Such an immediacy interpretation may well promote greater understanding of the client's strengths and deficits by helping this woman see how her feelings and situation are reflected in her every word and action. She may also realize that the practitioner is indeed "right there" with her all the time — and that the practitioner's concern is as genuine as it is immediate.

Practice Situations

In order to gain a further understanding of the skill of immediacy, read each of the client statements below. Then make an interpretation using the skill of immediacy.

> **Client 1 Statement:** *"My family doesn't understand what it's like to be on one of those wards. All the stuff that goes on. I mean, it's not their fault, they've never been there. But it sure makes me feel distant."*

The client is basically saying that anyone who has not been on a ward cannot understand the experience of being on a ward. Your response to immediacy should reflect the idea that the client is unsure whether you can really understand his or her experience. Now try to formulate an immediacy response to the second client.

Client 2 Statement: *"I really get mad when people think they're better. Just because they went to college or something doesn't make them any better."*

In this excerpt, the client is angry at people with degrees. Since you (as a rehabilitation practitioner) have a degree, you are included in this group. Your response should reflect the recognition that even now the client is angry with you because he or she believes you are looking down at him or her.

As you listen to your own clients, practice thinking about what each client is experiencing here and now with you. Try to formulate at least one immediacy interpretation per session. Be sure to note each client's reaction. He or she should appear to more involved with you at those moments.

Of course, there are times when a client's discussion of his or her situation is not related to the practitioner-client interaction — or even if it is, the client does not wish to acknowledge the fact. If a client reacts to an immediacy interpretation (or, for that matter, any other interpretation) by indicating that you were inaccurate or that she or he is not ready to hear the interpretation, simply respond to this reaction. For example: *"You feel annoyed with me because it seems as though I didn't understand you."* **No matter how brilliant and insightful you might think your interpretation is, it is not functional if the client cannot understand and agree with it!**

Confrontation

Responding with immediacy may be employed by the skilled practitioner at almost any point. It poses no threat to the client and can do much to facilitate greater understanding. Confrontations, however, are a different story. The effective practitioner may decide at some point that a client can be helped to understand something only through confrontation. This decision can never be made lightly. In the past, far too many practitioners have made frequent and often harmful use of confrontation. They have sought to "jolt" their clients into recognizing problems or deficits. Yet a review of the literature shows that *confrontation is neither a necessary nor a sufficient condition of effective diagnostic interviewing* (Berenson & Mitchell, 1974). At best, it is a tool the skilled practitioner uses cautiously if at all.

Confrontations may take a number of forms and may be prompted by any one of several practitioner perceptions. The practitioner may find that a given client is unwilling to abandon defensive "smoke screens." The practitioner may see a significant discrepancy between

75

what a client is saying and what he or she is doing. The practitioner may also perceive a discrepancy between how the client acts and how the client says she or he wants to act. Such discrepancies are identified by the practitioner by means of observing and listening skills.

There are, as noted, many ways of confronting a client. In general, however, these break down into two basic categories: *mild* confrontations and *strong* confrontations. In the first, the practitioner often employs a format along the lines of, *"On the one hand you say/feel/do* _____ *and on the other hand you say/feel/do* _____ ." Any practitioner considering using confrontation can begin by employing this mild approach, which focuses on the situation from the client's previous exploration. For example,

"On the one hand you say that you're looking forward to getting out of the hospital and on the other hand you say you're skipping your medication."

A mild confrontation of this sort is only minimally threatening to the client. It does focus on a discrepancy or element of contrast; but it does so in terms that come entirely from the client's own exploration of the situation.

In many cases, the accuracy of the practitioner's interchangeable responses at any given level makes confrontation unnecessary and undesirable. In other cases, mild confrontation may be all that is needed to promote greater understanding on the client's part. In a few cases, however, the practitioner may need to confront a client directly. Rather than limiting itself solely to what the client has disclosed to the practitioner, such a strong or direct confrontation stresses external and observable data. Here the format is usually a variation on, *"You say you feel/do* _____ *but it looks to me like you feel/do* _____ ." Before confronting a client directly like this, an effective practitioner must have paved the way by initiating a series of mild confrontations. Moreover, the practitioner can use the technique of direct confrontation only when there is ample observational data to back up any statement. No skilled practitioner, for example, would confront a client by saying, *"You say you feel confident, but that's baloney. You're really pretty unsure of yourself."* Besides being threatening in the extreme, such a statement reflects an arrogant, opinionated diagnosis rather than reality-based observational fact. In contrast, the following is a more facilitative confrontation:

"You say you feel confident, but your constant fidgeting and finger-drumming makes you look to me as though you're sort of nervous."

Here the practitioner has arrived at a diagnosis of the client's state by observing his or her nonverbal expressions.

Practice Situations

Again, read each of the client statements below. Then formulate an interpretation using the skill of confrontation.

Client 1

Background: Joan has an excellent high school record and has scored well on all the achievement tests she has taken in school.

Statement: *"I don't know about going to that X-ray technician school. I mean I'd really like it. But, you know, I don't think I can do well in school."*

Obviously there is a discrepancy between Joan's feeling of inadequacy in school and her past performance. A confrontation interpretation reflects this discrepancy.

It is important to note that the practitioner must sometimes confront the client with assets as well as with deficits.

Client 2

Background: Harold had indicated that he is really learning to stand up for his rights and focus his energy on accomplishing the things he has to do.

Statement: *"Boy! I'm really tired today. I'm going to school and have the part-time job. I also have to get up at four in the morning to drive Dad to work. I thought it was just going to be a week 'till my uncle got off vacation. But it's been two weeks now. I don't know when Dad's going to start riding with him again. 'Course I do live closer to him, and I guess Uncle Charles doesn't care to go out of his way.*

There is a discrepancy between the client's stated ability to stand up for himself and his actions of getting up at four in the morning to take his father to work. A confrontation interpretation reflects this discrepancy.

You should not simply practice looking for discrepancies with your clients. If you observe and/or hear discrepancies in a client's actions *and* if you believe you have a relationship that is sufficiently strong for the client's exploration and/or understanding to be facilitated by confrontation, then you can initiate a confrontation. Be sure, however, to respond to the client's reaction to the confrontation, particularly if she or he has trouble with it.

In the end, skilled practitioners always keep in mind the principles that guide and control the use of confrontation: *No practitioner con-*

fronts a client when there is an alternative approach that promises cli-ent gains; and no practitioner confronts a client directly when a mild confrontation might work as well.

MAKING A PERSONALIZED INTERPRETATION: A SUMMARY

Goal: To identify the client's specific strengths and weaknesses in re-lation to the rehabilitation goal.

1. Respond to the client's exploration.
2. Personalize the meaning of the client's situation.
3. Ask self: *"What is it that client cannot do that is causing him or her difficulties?"*

   or, in the case of strengths,

   Ask self: *"What is it that client can do that will help him or her overcome difficulties?"*
4. Identify a behavioral skill area in which the client is *deficient* (or, in the case of client strengths, *adequate*).
5. Share this behavioral skill area with the client by making a per-sonalized interpretive response, using a format similar to:

   "You feel _____ because you can't (need to) _____ ."

   or, in the case of strengths,

   "You feel _____ because you can _____ ."
6. If appropriate, make an interpretive response using immediacy or confrontation.

OBTAINING THE CLIENT'S SUGGESTIONS ABOUT PERSONALIZED STRENGTHS AND WEAKNESSES

There are many occasions when it is possible for *clients* to indicate what their strengths and weaknesses are in relation to their rehabilita-tion goal(s). Once the client and practitioner have identified the situa-tional problem(s) and rehabilitation goal(s), the client should be given the opportunity to identify his or her strong points and weak points. Practitioners do not always have to be the source of insights about their clients' skill behaviors.

The diagnostic planning process facilitates the client's willingness and ability to identify his or her own assets and deficits in several ways. First, when the practitioner responds accurately to the client's statements, the client is encouraged to speak honestly about him or her-self. This initial responsive stance of the practitioner provides the client with this opportunity to say whatever the client wants to say. At the same time, the client experiences a relationship in which he or she is being listened to and understood, rather than judged, analyzed, and questioned. As a result, the client will be more willing to talk personally about him or herself because the practitioner's responding has built a trusting relationship.

Another characteristic of the diagnostic planning process that facilitates the client's willingness and ability to discuss his or her strengths and weaknesses is the fact that the client's rehabilitation goals have first been specified in the diagnostics exploration phase. As a result, the client is encouraged to discuss his or her strengths and deficits *only with respect to the particular rehabilitation goal.* The client is not being asked to "bare his or her soul." The client is not being encouraged to discuss early childhood experiences nor his or her functioning with respect to the diagnostician's pet personality theory. Rather, the client is being asked to talk about him or herself only in relation to his or her own unique goal.

The final way in which the client's suggestions are facilitated is by the practitioner's direct encouragement of the client to become involved in the asset and deficit identification. The rehabilitation diagnostic process is not a mysterious process, but rather a process in which most clients can take an active role. Therefore, after the situational problems and rehabilitation goals have been specified, and the client has attempted to understand the personal meaning of his or her situation, the practitioner can specifically encourage the client to indicate what the client thinks his or her strong points or weak points are in relation to these goals. The practitioner can elicit client suggestions in a way similar to the following:

"Now that we know what goal we are aiming for and why it's important to you, the next task is to figure out what skills you have that will help you obtain this goal, and what skills you need to improve so that you can get to your goal. What do you think are some things you do well that will help you get to your goal? (What are some things you need to do better?)"

As the client suggests possible strengths and deficits, the practitioner responds so as to clarify what the client has said, as well as to identify any feelings the client may be expressing as he or she talks about strengths and deficits. For example, a client in a sheltered workshop might make the following statement about his deficits with respect to the goal of moving to a transitional employment setting:

Client: *"One thing that bothers me is that I'm not too good at meeting new people."*

Practitioner Response to Feeling and Content:
              "So you're somewhat apprehensive about your ability to get acquainted with people."

Client: *"I never had many friends at my other jobs."*

As the client tries to understand his or her specific strengths and deficits, the practitioner will want to encourage the client to verbally express descriptions of his or her skill behaviors. Most clients will not behaviorally describe the skill, so the practitioner must help the client identify the skill behavior that is implied in the client's comments. The following example is that of a young adult woman who is planning to resume her studies at a community college:

Client: "One thing I know I will have to do better this time is to spend more hours studying."

Practitioner Response to Content:
"You know you'll need to study more."

Client: "Last time I seemed to waste so much time — I always felt so disorganized."

Practitioner (attempting to identify the skill):
"It seems like you need to learn how to schedule your daily activities better."

Client: "I really do. I've never been very good at it."

Some clients are unable to suggest their own deficits or assets without additional encouragement. One tactic would be to have them first focus on their strengths in relation to their goals. Many clients find this an easier place to begin. Another practitioner strategy is for the practitioner to model what he or she wants the client to do by self-disclosing a practitioner strength and weakness in relation to one of the practitioner's goals. For example, the practitioner might say something like the following:

"Let me give you an example of what I want you to do. One of my goals is to someday be the director of an agency like this center. One of my strengths in relation to this goal is my public-speaking ability. One of the things I need to improve on is my ability to figure out a budget. What are some of your strong and weak points in relation to your rehabilitation goal?"

Practice Situations

Try role-playing with colleagues or friends with whom you already have an established relationship. First, identify a goal that they hope to achieve someday. (For this exercise, it is usually easiest to identify a career goal.) Ask them to identify their strengths and deficits in relation to this goal. Respond to their statements. Formulate their descriptions in more skill-based terms. If necessary, model this task by first self-disclosing a few of your own strengths and weaknesses in relation to a particular goal. After the exercise, evaluate how successful you were in getting your friend or colleague to make personalized statements.

Attempt to encourage your clients to become involved in making suggestions as to their strengths and weaknesses. Remember to first specify the goal and lay a responsive base with the client.

OBTAINING CLIENT SUGGESTIONS: A SUMMARY

Goal: To identify the client's specific strengths and weaknesses in relation to the rehabilitation goal.

1. Develop a responsive relationship with the client.
2. Specify the client's rehabilitation goal.
3. Ask the client to suggest strengths and deficits related to the rehabilitation goal.
4. If necessary, self-disclose one's own strengths and weaknesses as a model for what is expected of the client.

MAKING PRACTITIONER SUGGESTIONS ABOUT CLIENT'S STRENGTHS AND WEAKNESSES

Another way in which the practitioner can facilitate the client's identification of specific assets and deficits is by directly suggesting them to the client. This method of personalizing differs from practitioner personalized interpretations in that the suggestions do not flow directly out of the client's exploration. Rather, these suggestions are based on either the practitioner's previous experience with clients who have had similar goals, or based on information obtained from test data.

The rehabilitation diagnostician defines what is meant by a "test" in its very broadest terms. A test situation includes not only the typical paper and pencil tests but any situation in which the practitioner's goal is to gather information about the client's strengths and deficits. Thus, "tests" would include observations of the client made in real-world situations, observations of the client made in simulated situations (e.g., work samples), and observations of the client in role-played situations.

This text is not designed to equip the practitioner with testing skills; other books are helpful in achieving that purpose. However, there are several points concerning testing of which the rehabilitation diagnostician will want to be aware. First, testing procedures are only used to gather information that is specific to the client's situational problems and rehabilitation goals. Rehabilitation diagnosticians do not administer an overall test battery as a routine way of collecting data about the client's functioning. Instead, rehabilitation diagnosticians use test situations to answer very specific questions about a client's strengths and weaknesses with respect to certain goals.

For example, a rehabilitation practitioner might be working with Mr. Jones, a client being treated for alcoholism. A typical type of test battery given by other practitioners might include personality tests, intelligence tests, and tests for organic impairment. Yet it is not sufficient for the rehabilitation practitioner to know that Mr. Jones is functioning in the average range of intelligence, that his verbal IQ is forty points higher than his performance IQ, that his behavior is passive-aggressive, and that his immediate recall is poor. Rather, the test information can be used to answer the question: "Given Mr. Jones's rehabilitation goals, what skills is he likely to be able to perform or not perform." Mr. Jones is a policeman who enjoys "working the beat." He has no aspirations to be anything else. His "average" intellectual functioning is most likely to be sufficient for him to be able to observe events, analyze what he sees, and make immediate action decisions. The discrepancy between verbal IQ and performance IQ suggests organic impairment. This is further substantiated by the poor memory functioning. However, a diagnosis of "organicity" conveys little information about a person's *skills*. Further testing needs to be done to pinpoint what *functions* are impaired: Coordination? Spatial judgment? Ability to retain new learning? Without such details, it is impossible to relate the test findings to the stated rehabilitation goals of getting Mr. Jones back to work. It is possible for Mr. Jones to have some organic impairment that has no relevance to his police duties. He may have a perceptual problem that causes him to reverse his letters ("p's" and "b's"). This would have little effect on his performance of job functions. Also, of what use to the rehabilitation practitioner is that information about Mr. Jones's passive-aggressiveness? In exploring with Mr. Jones, the rehabilitation practitioner can use this information to guide the direction of the interview. Does Mr. Jones have difficulty expressing his resentments directly? Is he aware of "getting back" at his fellow officers or community in indirect ways that leave him unsatisfied and more likely to drink? Does he know alternative behaviors? Even traditional types of testing, when shared with the client to explore for skills, can be a useful tool in furthering client exploration and understanding.

It must be remembered that the value of any test information, no matter what the source, is greatly diminished if the practitioner cannot share the information with the client in such a way that the client agrees with and understands the test data. Esoteric terminology must be avoided. Furthermore, the practitioner will often want to translate the information into phraseology that explicitly identifies specific strengths and deficits. Lastly, when the practitioner shares this information with the client, she or he will want to be certain to respond to the client so as to check out the client's understanding and agreement. The client needs to "own" the test information just as the client needs to "own" the practitioner's personalized interpretations. The client must move from a perception of "the test said this about me" to an experience of "so these are my strengths and deficits that the test situations helped us discover."

The client's willingness to accept practitioner suggestions made from test data is in great part a function of what events have preceded the suggestions. Test data are introduced only after a relationship has been developed, the rehabilitation goals have been specified, and the client has first had the opportunity to make his or her own suggestions as to particular strengths and deficits.

In addition to test data, the practitioner has another source of information from which to draw for the purpose of suggesting additional strengths and deficits. That is, the practitioner's prior experience in working with clients who have been in similar situations. Based on this prior experience, the practitioner will probably be aware of important skill areas that neither the client's previous exploration nor test information has uncovered.

For example, a psychiatric rehabilitation practitioner might have learned, based on previous experiences with psychiatrically disabled clients, that many recently discharged inpatients are unable to or afraid of answering questions about their previous hospitalization. This may occur in any environmental area, for example, with neighbors, school admission personnel, and/or fellow employees. Furthermore, it is a skill deficit area of which many clients are unaware until the situation directly confronts them. And when it does, their inability is often evidenced by apologies, stammering or negative remarks about themselves or the experience, which only serve to make the client look less normal or capable. Such a client is lacking the skill of "stigma reduction"; a psychiatric rehabilitation practitioner could introduce this deficit area to a client in a manner similar to the following:

"There is another skill that I think might be important. The behavior I'm talking about is 'stigma reduction.' I have found that many clients in your particular situation have difficulty performing this skill. What I mean by 'stigma-reducing behavior' is the ability to answer questions that people might ask about your hospital experience, without saying anything negative about yourself."

The practitioner and the client can then discuss the behavior further until the client indicates understanding of the behavior and agreement that it is a critical behavior for the situation. Then the practitioner and the client can decide whether the behavior is in fact a strength or a deficit. Test situations, such as real-world observations, simulations, or role-plays may be used at this point to assist in the determination of whether the behavior is a strength or a deficit. For example, the client's stigma-reduction skills can be determined by the practitioner role-playing a neighbor (or employment interviewer, etc.) and asking the client, "Why were you hospitalized?" The client's answer will indicate whether he or she has stigma-reduction skills.

For each new behavioral skill that the practitioner introduces, the practitioner must explain what he or she means by that behavior. The practitioner's direct suggestion of certain skill behaviors this late in the diagnostic planning process is deliberate. For one reason, by this time the practitioner and the client have had the time in which to develop a positive relationship. As a result the client should be more amenable to listening to the practitioner's description of the skill and agreeing with the practitioner's suggestions. For another reason, up to this point the diagnostic emphasis deliberately has been on understanding the client's skills based on the client's own unique situation. This has resulted in the client and practitioner together identifying a number of critical skill behaviors. Thus, many strength or deficit behaviors that the practitioner might have had to otherwise directly suggest have already been developed out of a cooperative effort.

Practice Situations

You can practice this skill in the same role-play situation that was used to try to practice getting a client to make suggestions about his or her strengths and deficits. After your colleague or friend who is role-playing with you has identified some of her or his own strengths and deficits in relation to a specific goal, try to suggest additional skill behaviors that might be critical in achieving this goal. By using your responding skills (responding to feeling, to content, and with questions), try to have the person reach an understanding of whether the skill is a strength or deficit. If necessary, create a test situation that can assist the person in determining whether the behavior is a strength or deficit.

With your clients, after the appropriate groundwork has been laid, make suggestions as to what skill behaviors you think might be critical in the attainment of their goals. Use testing situations and client exploration to identify whether the client does or does not have those critical skills. Remember to be responsive to the client's attempts at personalized understanding.

MAKING PRACTITIONER SUGGESTIONS: A SUMMARY

Goal: To identify the client's specific strengths and weaknesses in relation to the rehabilitation goal.

1. Develop a responsive relationship with the client.
2. Specify the client's rehabilitation goal.
3. Obtain client suggestions about strengths and weaknesses.
4. Gather the needed "test" information about the client's strengths and weaknesses relevant to the rehabilitation goal;

    and/or

5. Identify skill strengths and weaknesses common to clients with this type of rehabilitation goal.

6. Suggest to the client these possible skill strengths and weaknesses.

7. Describe these skills to the client as behaviorally as possible.

8. Make certain to respond to the client's comments about your suggestions.

SHARING SIGNIFICANT OTHERS' SUGGESTIONS ABOUT CLIENT STRENGTHS AND WEAKNESSES

Another typical method in which the practitioner can obtain information about the client's strengths and weaknesses is by interviewing significant others in the client's life. These persons (e.g., relatives, friends, other treatment personnel, employers, etc.) have had a chance to observe the client in many different environments. They represent a valuable source of information for the practitioner about the client's abilities.

Because the involvement of significant others is such a critical part of the diagnostic planning process, this text will discuss this issue in a separate chapter (see Chapter 5). What needs to be mentioned at this point is that the suggestions of significant others can be dealt with in the same manner as the practitioner's suggestions that were based on the practitioner's previous experience or from test data. That is, the information from significant others about client strengths and weaknesses must be shared with the client. Similarly, in order for this information to have significant treatment value, the client must understand and be in agreement with these suggestions. Like suggestions from other sources, this "owning" process is greatly enhanced by what has occurred previously. That is, this information is shared with the client only after a practitioner-client relationship has been established, the situational problem(s) and rehabilitation goal(s) have been specified, and the client has already suggested some critical personal strengths and deficits.

ASSESSING THE CLIENT'S LEVEL OF PERSONALIZING

It is possible to keep track of the level of client exploration and understanding by means of the five-point scale presented in Table 12. Using this scale, the practitioner can assess the client's level of exploration or understanding in any given area of concern. This assessment can indicate to the practitioner how far along the diagnostic process is at any given moment. A rating of level 1.0 indicates that the client is *not involved* in the interview process. The next two levels (2.0 and 3.0) indicate *increasing levels of self-exploration,* while the final two levels (4.0 and 5.0) describe *increasing levels of client understanding.* Noting the client's level of self-exploration can help the practitioner know how to react to the client. For example, to clients at level 1.0, a response to content might be most appropriate. As another example, clients should be exploring at level 3.0 before the practitioner introduces personalized responses.

The same client can be at different levels of the scale depending upon what particular topic is being discussed. An institutionalized patient, for example, might be discussing returning to her or his former living environment at a personalized level (4.0 or 5.0) but only talking about returning to work at a content level (2.0).

Table 12. Client Diagnostic Interviewing Scale

Level 1.0   The client *does not discuss any relevant material.* He or she either does not express himself or herself at all or talks only about situations that have no relevance to the rehabilitation situation.

Level 2.0   The client *discusses material about relevant situations.* He or she explores the who, what, where, when, why and how of the particular situation.

Level 3.0   The client *discusses material about relevant situations and his or her feelings* concerning these situations. He or she explores this material with emotional proximity (i.e., says things the way he or she feels them).

Level 4.0   The client *discusses material concerning the personal meaning* of the situations with which he or she is faced. That is, the client talks about why the experiences she or he is having are personally important. Again, he or she explores this material with emotional proximity.

Level 5.0   The client *discusses material concerning the personalized strengths and deficits* she or he has. That is, the client works to identify the specific personal strengths or deficits relevant to her or his rehabilitation situation. The client's attempts to understand this material are marked by emotional proximity.

There is also variance between clients in terms of this scale. Most clients begin the diagnostic interview process at level 1.0 or 2.0. Other clients begin by discussing their situation and their feelings about it (level 3.0). On rarer occasions, clients may begin by discussing what their situation means to them (level 4.0) or what personal strengths or deficits are most relevant to their situation (level 5.0). However, even those clients who start the rehabilitation process at a more personalized level may not necessarily understand their specific strengths and deficits in relation to their rehabilitation goals. They just may be more open to owning their own responsibility for doing something about their problems. For the most part, however, it is the skills of the rehabilitation practitioner that facilitate client movement to higher scale levels. As suggested above, the rehabilitation practitioner attempts to move the client to the next higher level when the client has been able to sustain a discussion at a given scale level. For example, when a client is able to discuss his or her working situation and the feelings she or he has about it without relying on the practitioner for stimulation, the client is indicating to the practitioner that she or he is open to considering the personal meaning of the situation.

The practitioner may find it difficult to get some very low-level functioning clients to personalize meaning, strengths, and deficits. Unfortunately, if the client cannot understand his or her own personal role in the rehabilitation process, it will be very difficult to get the client initially involved in any subsequent rehabilitation treatment program. In such cases, a rehabilitation intervention will probably have to be made *from only the practitioner's understanding* of the client's personal strengths and deficits. Once this intervention is made, the client may then become involved in a more structured exploration and understanding of the specific environmental setting in which he or she has been placed.

CATEGORIZING THE CLIENT'S STRENGTHS AND DEFICITS

During the personalizing process, the practitioner and client are developing a list of relevant strengths and weaknesses. Using this list of client assets and deficits, the practitioner and client can proceed directly to the assessment stage of the diagnostic planning process. During this assessment stage, each identified skill behavior is objectively defined (or operationalized) and then the client's present and needed level of functioning is determined. These assessment steps complete the diagnostic planning process.

However, instead of proceeding to the assessment stage with only a list of critical client skills, the practitioner can first organize the list of identified skill behaviors in a way that maximizes diagnostic *understanding* and *comprehensiveness*. Simply possessing a list of client strengths and deficits does not completely portray a client's overall unique pattern of strengths and weaknesses. The diagnosed skill behaviors can be depicted in a way that facilitates the client's understanding of how he or she is functioning with respect to his or her rehabilitation goals. In addition, the identified client skills can be portrayed in a way that assures that the diagnosis has been as thorough and comprehensive as was needed.

In order to achieve both diagnostic understanding and comprehensiveness, the rehabilitation diagnostic model attempts to organize the diagnostic information along two major dimensions: (1) the classification of the client's skill behaviors as to whether the skills are physical, emotional, or intellectual skills; and (2) the classification of the environments in which these client skill behaviors are exhibited as to whether the environment is either a living, learning, or working setting. This simple method of organizing the diagnostic information facilitates both the client's and treatment personnel's understanding of the diagnostic data as well as assures a comprehensive diagnosis. In terms of comprehensiveness, by classifying the client's skills into physical, emotional, and intellectual categories, the practitioner insures that every conceivable client skill behavior has the potential of being diagnosed. Historically, diagnoses have not been comprehensive and, as a result, the psychiatrically disabled client's physical functioning has been almost totally ignored. In neglecting the client's level of physical functioning, practitioners in psychiatric rehabilitation have ignored an area in which psychiatrically disabled clients often perform poorly, an area that affects both emotional and intellectual areas of functioning, and an area that, by virtue of its concreteness, can provide valuable skill generalizations to other areas of functioning (Vitalo & Farkas, 1979). The practice of psychiatric rehabilitation assumes a relationship between a person's physical, intellectual, and emotional functioning; therefore, a thorough diagnostic plan must ensure that each of these areas has been included in the plan.

In addition, the development of an organized, comprehensive diagnostic picture is clearly mandated by the research that suggests that client functioning in one environmental area is not consistently correlated with functioning in other environments. Thus, we see psychiatrically disabled clients who are working successfully having to return to the hospital because of problems at home; or clients who are adjusting well to a living environment yet cannot find or hold a job; or clients performing well in a learning environment who are still unable to hold a part-time job or relate well to family and friends at home (Anthony, Buell, Sharratt, & Althoff, 1972). Another reason for the necessity of a comprehensive diagnosis of the client's functioning is that many psychiatrically disabled clients have numerous rehabilitation needs. As a result, many different treatment personnel are involved in rehabilitating the client. A comprehensive and understandable diagnostic picture of the client can facilitate the efforts of this rehabilitation team approach. In contrast, the absence of such a diagnostic picture can result in both duplication of treatment effort as well as the unintentional neglect of certain client rehabilitation needs.

Thus, because such a categorization process can maximize thoroughness and minimize misunderstandings, it is recommended that the practitioner first categorize the list of strengths and deficits before proceeding to the next diagnostic stage. The Client Diagnostic Plan-

Table 13.
Client Diagnostic Planning Chart

Name _____

Situational Problem: _____

Rehabilitation Goal: _____

Environment	Strength / Deficit	Physical Skills	Emotional Skills	Intellectual Skills
Living	+			
	−			
Learning	+			
	−			
Working	+			
	−			

ning Chart, which was illustrated in Table 1 and is pictured again in Table 13, is an effective tool for recording the diagnosed strengths and deficits. The format of the chart allows the practitioner to categorize the client's strengths and deficits with respect to whether they are physical, emotional, or intellectual skills and with respect to whether these skills are used in the client's living, learning, or working environment.

CATEGORIZING BY CLIENT SKILL AREAS

Categorizing the client's skill strengths and deficits in terms of physical, intellectual, and emotional behaviors is a process that most clients can comprehend. Thus, the client can take an active and often enthusiastic role in this phase of the diagnostic planning process. The need for this step in the diagnostic plan can be explained to the client in a manner similar to the following:

"Now that we have identified some of the things (strengths and deficits) that are important in your rehabilitation plan, let's list them in a way that will give us an overall picture of your strengths and weaknesses. We will try to categorize each of these behaviors in terms of whether it is primarily a physical behavior, an intellectual behavior, or an emotional behavior."

The practitioner can then show the client how one of the client's behaviors can be categorized as a physical skill, how another can be categorized as an intellectual skill, and how still another can be categorized as an emotional skill behavior. A skill behavior is categorized as physical (P) if the primary part of the skill performance involves some specific physical behavior. When the primary part of the behavior involves thinking or mental activity, the behavior is categorized as an intellectual skill (I). A skill is categorized as emotional (E) if the primary behavior involves relating to people.

Table 14 lists a variety of client skill behaviors under the categories physical, emotional, and intellectual (PEI). Obviously, some clients may not have discussed skill behaviors in a particular P, E, or I area; or all skill behaviors identified so far might be in one area. Also, clients will vary in terms of the number of listed skill areas, with some clients possessing only a few identified strengths and weaknesses while other clients may have identified strengths and deficits going into the double figures. The final step of the diagnostic categorization process will provide the practitioner with an opportunity to review and, if necessary, add to the skills list. Initially, however, the practitioner's major focus is on developing the diagnostic picture based on the information as it evolves during the personalizing process.

Table 14.

Sample Client Skill Behaviors Classified P, E, and I

PHYSICAL	EMOTIONAL	INTELLECTUAL
being well groomed	disciplining children	remembering directions
losing weight	controlling temper with spouse	giving directions
lifting heavy things	controlling temper with co-workers	giving a speech
being punctual	responding to spouse's feelings	asking questions of teacher
playing a sport	making eye contact with others	following directions
learning a new sport	staying calm at job interviews	balancing a checkbook
learning a physical fitness regimen	making friends	reading newspaper
being sexually active	talking on telephone	writing letters to family
doing housework	going to parties	making decisions with family
doing yardwork	having parties	seeking a job
driving a car	explaining problems to others	asking for a raise
using public transportation	differentially reinforcing others	learning a hobby
getting to sleep	teaching children manners	cooking
getting up	listening to others	using services of public agencies
standing for long periods	making accurate observations	setting goals for self
sitting for long periods	giving directions	reinforcing self
attending to the instructor	showing affection to family	writing programs for self
climbing up stairs	conversing with fellow workers	brainstorming alternatives
making home repairs	accepting criticism from boss	memorizing an answer
eating nutritious foods	speaking during group discussion	choosing a job
not engaging in "institutional	calling in when feeling suicidal	studying a book
behaviors" (e.g., rolling fingers)	discriminating hallucination from a	reading quickly
developing finger dexterity	real experience	typing papers
developing gross motor control		writing papers
		listing realistic job alternatives
		planning a career route

Practice Situations

In Table 15 is a list of client strengths and deficits developed from a diagnostic interview. Categorize this list into PEI Categories by placing each deficit in the appropriate cell in Table 16. Note that some behaviors may be more difficult to classify than others and that a few of the behaviors may seem to fall equally as well into two or three categories. For these behaviors, simply classify each in the category that already has the most skills listed, as this is probably the area that is playing a fundamental role in the client's rehabilitation situation.

Another way in which you can practice categorizing skill behavior is to think of as many such behaviors as you can that you yourself perform each day. As you think of each skilled behavior, place it in the appropriate category in Table 17. It is fairly easy to generate these skilled behaviors by thinking of the tasks you perform each day and the skills that you use to accomplish those tasks.

Table 15. A List of Client Skill Behaviors Classified P, E, and I

Skill Strengths

Reads daily newspaper
Bowls weekly
Can perform intellectual duties of job (selling apliances)
Can make friends at work
Can attend to customers' presence

Skill Deficits

Spends no time with one-year-old child
Cannot stand at work for long periods of time
Cannot get to sleep at night
Does not compliment spouse
Has below-average physical fitness regimen
Cannot positively acknowledge compliments of spouse
Has not made any friends in his apartment building or immediate
    neighborhood
Cannot involve self with any activities but TV during weekends
Does not eat balanced diet
Cannot get to places on time

Table 16.
Client Skill Behaviors Classified P, E, and I

	Physical	Emotional	Intellectual
Strengths			
Deficits			

Table 17.
Your List of Skill Behaviors Classified P, E, and I

	Physical	Emotional	Intellectual
Strengths			
Deficits			

The skill list that you and others develop will give you insights into the amazing number and variety of skills that you perform each day. Each of these skill behaviors represents possible client strengths and deficits and any single one or a combination of several may be enough to facilitate or destroy a client's rehabilitation outcome. The sheer magnitude of skilled behaviors that are performed each day in order to live, learn, and/or work in the community reflects the need for a comprehensive diagnosis. The small number of skill categories (PEI), the familiarity of the skill behaviors, and the deliberate absence of esoteric language maximize the possibility of clients becoming involved in the categorization process.

As a final step in learning to categorize client skill areas, attempt to categorize (as in Table 16) the deficits and strengths of one of your current clients. Try to involve the client in the process as much as possible by explaining the categorization process and having the client suggest how various behaviors might be classified. The constant concern of the rehabilitation practitioner is to guard against the client becoming a passive recipient of a diagnostic plan that she or he neither agrees with nor understands.

CATEGORIZING BY ENVIRONMENTAL AREAS

A thorough and understandable picture of a client's rehabilitation needs can be obtained by classifying the client's physical, emotional, and intellectual strengths and deficits in terms of the particular environmental area(s) in which the behaviors are facilitating or restricting the client's functioning. Here the practitioner and the client can see not only which particular client skill area(s) is critical but also which particular environments will be affected by the client's previously diagnosed skills.

The settings within which the psychiatrically disabled client functions may be classified as living, learning, and working environments. The purpose of dividing the client's environments into these three categories is to achieve a truly comprehensive picture of the client's skilled behaviors. These three environmental categories of living (L), learning (L), and working (W) constitute the total possible environments within which clients function. Every skilled behavior a client performs can be classified in one or more of these environmental areas.

In terms of comprehensibility, the words *living, learning, and working* (LLW) are simple ones with relatively straightforward meanings capable of being understood by most clients. The rehabilitation practitioner can explain to the client that living environments include those environments in which the client resides or plays (e.g., home, apartment, a recreational facility, a neighborhood, etc.). Learning environments are those places that are primarily educational in nature (high schools, universities, adult education settings, museums, libraries, etc.)

where one learns physical, emotional, and intellectual skills. Working environments are those settings in which the primary tasks are work-related (competitive employment, workshops, sheltered employment settings, etc.). Clearly, some settings combine features of two or more environments. For example, while the primary activity of a workshop is work-related, the work experience as well as some of the ancillary experiences are also educational in nature.

The particular environmental settings of interest are first identified when the client's situational problem(s) and rehabilitation goal(s) are specified during the exploration process. At that time, the particular situation (or environment) in which the client is experiencing difficulty is specifically identified. Many agencies specialize in particular environmental areas. Thus, there are, for example, halfway houses and day treatment centers (living), special classes or schools for the "emotionally disturbed" (learning), sheltered workshops and vocational rehabilitation agencies (working). As a result, many practitioners initially focus their diagnosis of client strengths and deficits in terms of their specialty environment. These settings are expected (and sometimes mandated) to focus their treatment intervention on the client's functioning in one type of environment. Unfortunately, however, even though their mission is clearly defined in one environmental area, their client's functioning is not compartmentalized. A vocational agency's attempts to return a client to competitive employment is often hindered by the client's problems at home; the client's functioning in a school setting might be similarly hampered by poor relationships in the living environment; or, a client's adjustment to a residential setting might be upset by an inability to work productively during the day. Thus, it makes sense for the rehabilitation practitioners to diagnose client functioning in environmental areas outside their sphere of influence. If they themselves cannot treat those deficits diagnosed in other environmental areas, they can refer the client to someone who specializes in the other environment. To ignore these other client areas of functioning is to court failure. Although agencies' treatment expertise may be limited to specific environments, their diagnostic expertise must not be so limited. During a thorough diagnostic process, the practitioner will often learn of client strengths and deficits in environments that are not of primary relevance to the rehabilitation goal but that *still may affect the clients' functioning in their environment of interest.*

In addition, it is often during the personalizing stage of the diagnostic planning process that new environments of interest might be suggested. For example, a client who is hoping to obtain employment might need to first return to school to obtain the needed credentials. The client's strengths and deficits in relation to a learning environment must then be diagnosed. Or a client whose goal is to leave the hospital and live in the only available residential setting may be required by the residence to work in a sheltered setting during part of the day. The client's assets and weaknesses in relation to a sheltered employment setting must then be diagnosed.

By organizing the client's PEI skill behaviors into LLW environmental areas, the rehabilitation practitioner (working as closely as possible with the client) can develop a picture of how the client's functioning in each environmental area will be affected by the client's unique pattern of PEI strengths and deficits. Table 18 graphically illustrates how the client skills that were previously identified and classified PEI in Table 14 can be classified again in terms of which LLW environments these skills will affect. This example is not derived from any specific client but serves mainly as an illustration of how some typical client behaviors are often categorized.

This simple PEI × LLW classification scheme eliminates much of the confusion that has heretofore interfered with attempts to categorize client skill functioning. Previous classification attempts have confused client *skills* with the *environments* in which the clients use their skills. Thus, an incorrect categorization might classify a client's skills in the following way: social skills, vocational skills, leisure skills, intellectual skills, and physical skills. In contrast, the rehabilitation diagnostic categories presented in this text avoid any confusion of skill and environment. The skills reside in the client and are categorized as physical, emotional, and intellectual. The environments reflect real-world settings and are categorized as living, learning, and working. Thus, for example, a client can exhibit the physical skill of punctuality by arriving on time for meals (living environment), adult education class (learning environment), and/or his or her job (working environment).

The diagnostic picture that emerges when specific clients are diagnosed will begin to give the practitioner and the client an idea of which environmental areas are strongest and which are weakest and of how certain client skill behaviors are manifested in only certain environmental areas. For example, a client may possess a number of physical deficits that prevent him or her from performing in a particular working environment yet may have only physical strengths when it comes to a learning environment; or a client may have many emotional deficits in the living area but none in the working area. As the diagnostic picture of the client begins to emerge, the practitioner will begin to see various rehabilitation treatment implications. However, the diagnostic plan is not complete until the third stage of the diagnostic planning process (the assessment stage) has also been accomplished.

Practice Situations

In Table 19 is the list of client strengths and deficits that you classified PEI in Table 16. Now classify these skills again in terms of environmental areas by placing each PEI strength or deficit in the appropriate LLW cell. Use a format similar to Table 20 to record these skills. Assume

Table 18.
Client Skill Behaviors Classified Both P, E, and I and L, L, and W

	Physical	Emotional	Intellectual
Living	being well groomed losing weight being punctual playing a sport being sexually active housework yardwork driving a car using public transportation getting to sleep getting up making home repairs eating nutritious foods not engaging in "institutional behaviors"	disciplining children controlling temper with spouse responding to spouse's feelings making eye contact with others making friends talking on telephone going to parties having parties explaining problems to others differentially reinforcing others teaching children manners showing affection to family	balancing a checkbook reading a newspaper writing letters to family making decisions with family learning a hobby cooking using services of public agencies setting goals for self reinforcing self writing program for self brainstorming alternatives
Learning	being punctual learning a new sport learning a physical fitness regimen sitting for long periods attending to the instructor	making friends listening making accurate observations speaking during group discussion	asking questions of teacher following directions giving a speech learning a hobby memorizing answers studying a book reading quickly typing papers writing papers
Working	being well groomed lifting heavy things being punctual driving a car using public transportation standing for long periods climbing up stairs finger dexterity gross motor control	controlling temper with co-workers making friends listening making accurate observations conversing with fellow workers accepting criticism of boss	remembering directions giving directions following directions seeking a job asking for a raise choosing a job listing realistic job alternatives planning a career route

that the client's living environment is his apartment with a wife and child; that his learning environment is a physical fitness class at the local Y; and that his working environment is a department store. The client's situational problem is that he is unemployed and living at a halfway house. His rehabilitation goal is to live at home and work as an appliance salesman. Indicate the problems and goals at the top of the page and the specific environments in the left margin of the appropriate cell. A few skills may appear in every environmental area; most are specific to only one environmental area. Table 20 is a Client Diagnostic Planning Chart. At this stage in the diagnostic planning process, this chart summarizes in a comprehensive and understandable way the client's unique pattern of strengths and deficits in relation to the rehabilitation goals.

Additional practice in categorizing skill behaviors can be obtained by recategorizing into LLW environments your own PEI skilled activities, which you listed in Table 17. Place these on a Diagnostic Planning Chart in the appropriate cells, selecting the asset or deficit cell depending upon whether you are pleased or displeased with your present level of functioning.

Table 19. A List of Client P, E, and I Skill Strengths and Deficits to Be Classified L, L, and W

Skill Strengths
(I) Reads daily newspaper
(P) Bowls weekly
(I) Can perform intellectual duties of job (selling appliances)
(E) Can make friends at work
(E) Can attend to customers' presence

Skill Deficits
(E) Spends no time with one-year-old child
(P) Cannot stand at work for long periods of time
(P) Cannot get to sleep at night
(E) Does not compliment spouse
(P) Below-average physical fitness regimen
(E) Cannot positively acknowledge compliments of spouse
(E) Has not made any friends in his apartment building or immediate neighborhood
(I) Client cannot involve self with any activities but TV during weekends
(P) Does not eat balanced diet
(P) Cannot get to places on time

Table 20.

Client P, E, and I Skill Strengths (+) and Deficits (–) Classified L, L, and W

CLIENT DIAGNOSTIC PLANNING CHART   Name _____

Situational Problem: _____

Rehabilitation Goal: _____

Environment	Strength / Deficit	Physical Skills	Emotional Skills	Intellectual Skills
Living	+			
	–			
Learning	+			
	–			
Working	+			
	–			

Now practice categorizing your own client's skills PEI x LLW. Place these skills on the Diagnostic Planning Chart presented earlier. Attempt to involve each client in this process as much as possible. Once again, because of the small number of categories, the familiarity of the activities, and the concreteness of the language, the involvement of most clients should be ensured. By the time the diagnostic chart is completed, the client as well as the practitioner should be starting to gain an initial understanding of some of the things that will have to be done in order to achieve rehabilitation success.

In actual practice, the practitioner typically categorizes a particular skill along both dimensions (PEI skills by LLW environments) at the same time. That is, when a diagnosed skill is placed in the appropriate cell on the Diagnostic Planning Chart, this cell placement simultaneously indicates whether the skill is physical, intellectual, or emotional and whether it is relevant to the client's living, learning, or working environment.

Once the practitioner has learned the skills of this understanding stage of the diagnostic process, he or she may begin to use the Diagnostic Planning Chart during the early phases of this understanding stage. Thus, when several strengths and deficits have been diagnosed, the practitioner may, at that time, wish to begin recording them on the Diagnostic Planning Chart. The introduction of the chart can serve to increase the chart's involvement in the diagnostic task, reduce unnecessary confusion, and make the process more goal-directed. The earliest the Diagnostic Planning Chart can be introduced into the process is after the situational problems and rehabilitation goals have been specified. These are then recorded on the top of the Diagnostic Planning Chart.

Another advantage of introducing the Diagnostic Planning Chart relatively early in the understanding stage is that it keeps the focus on diagnosis rather than on premature problem-solving. So often the client (and sometimes the practitioner) tries to suggest solutions (or programs) before the client's strengths and deficits have been accurately diagnosed. The Diagnostic Planning Chart serves to emphasize that the initial eforts must be devoted to diagnosis, so that the treatment programs that do emerge will be comprehensive and tailored to the client's unique situation.

There may be times when the practitioner may not wish to use the Diagnostic Planning Chart in its entirety. Perhaps the learning and/or working environments may never be applicable for certain clients. In those instances, the practitioner can simply construct a chart depicting physical, intellectual, and emotional categories in the living environment.

The key point to remember about the Diagnostic Planning Chart is that it is simply a diagnostic tool. Its effectiveness is to a great extent a function of the interviewing skills of the diagnostic interviewer. However, when it is used by a skilled interviewer, it does bring certain advantages to the diagnostic planning process: (1) it maximizes diagnostic comprehensiveness; (2) it maximizes diagnostic understanding — for the client, significant others, and the practitioner; (3) it facilitates understanding of the client's diagnosis among various rehabilitation team members; (4) it makes the diagnostic process less confusing and more goal-directed; and (5) it maximizes the client's involvement in the process. Even if the client approaches the task as an intellectual exercise, the practitioner can try to facilitate the client's emotional involvement by responding to any hint of a feeling or by summarizing what the entire diagnostic planning process may have personally meant to the client.

REVIEWING THE SKILL BEHAVIORS TO ENSURE UNDERSTANDING AND COMPREHENSIVENESS

The final step in the categorization process is, in actuality, a "check-step" to make sure that the diagnostic categorization process has been both understandable and comprehensive. This is accomplished by *reviewing* with the client the specific skills listed on the Diagnostic Planning Chart and then, if necessary, *expanding* the quantity of skills listed by systematically examining whether or not there are any other important skill behaviors that need to be included on the chart. This check on the effectiveness of the categorization process is an important prerequisite to actually *assessing* these deficit areas. This last assessment stage of diagnostic planning is greatly facilitated if the practitioner has checked to make sure that the diagnosis has been comprehensive and that the client understands the complete diagnostic overview. Thus, it makes sense at some point during the categorizing phase to deliberately recheck the client's understanding of the skill behaviors and how they are categorized. Although this checking process has occurred routinely while the practitioner and client were developing the chart, it is important to take the time to review the diagnosis in its entirety — both for the purposes of client and practitioner understandability and as a means of possibly expanding the number of diagnosed skills.

The ability to understand the diagnosis will obviously vary among individual clients. However, if the practitioner has been careful to keep the language simple and to check the clients' understanding periodically as the diagnostic charts were being developed, most clients should be able to understand the completed charts.

The importance of this review process has been underlined by a recent research study (Bolton, 1978) that investigated the extent of agreement between counselors and rehabilitation clients with respect to the client's assessed needs. The results indicate that there was only modest agreement between the viewpoints of the counselor and the client. Particularly surprising was the finding of only modest agreement on assessment items that seemed relatively objective. Results such as these serve to stress the importance of the practitioner checking out with the client their mutual understanding of the client skill behaviors that have been identified.

The first step in the reviewing process is to introduce the task of reviewing the diagnosis to the client. This should include the *what* and *why* of reviewing the chart. That is, the practitioner can briefly describe to the client what the practitioner wishes to accomplish in reviewing the diagnostic charts and why it is important. Then she or he can pause and check out whether the client understands the task.

The introduction to the review process may be similar to the following:
"Now let's go over these charts to see if we both understand what we have listed. We want to be sure that we both have an idea of what skill areas might be important in your rehabilitation."

Specifically, the *what* here is "going over" or reviewing the charts; the *why* is "to see if we both understand or have an idea of what skill areas might be important in your rehabilitation."

Once the practitioner has ascertained that the client understands the purpose of the review, the practitioner can indicate *how* the review will be accomplished. The practitioner accomplishes this by *telling* the client exactly what needs to be done, *showing* the client an example of the task being done, and then structuring the situation as necessary so that the client ends up *doing* the task.

The practitioner can *tell* the client what needs to be done in a manner similar to the following:
"In order to make sure that we understand what might be important, we will discuss the strengths and deficits in each particular area. Then, when we think we have a pretty good idea of what we mean by each particular skill, we will place our initials next to that skill."

The practitioner can then *show* the client what needs to be done in a manner similar to the following:
"For example, the first skill deficit listed in the physical area/living environment is 'helping spouse with household tasks.' What this means to me is that you need to increase the number of tasks that you do around the house. Now if you and I both agree that this is essentially what we mean by this behavior, we can each place our initials next to this behavior."

The practitioner can then arrange for the client to *do* the tasks by saying something similar to the following:
"Now I would like you to explain to me what you think we mean by each of the remaining behaviors on this chart. I'll help with any that are giving you trouble. After we each indicate that we understand what is meant by each behavior, we can place our initials next to it. Let's start

with the next behavior in the physical area/living environment. What does that behavior mean to you?"

Obviously, different clients will need differing amounts of structure for this task. However, the point is that this diagnostic planning step allows for a reexploration of the client's understanding of what skills are relevant for achieving a successful rehabilitation outcome. Thus, the practitioner is constantly using his or her diagnostic interviewing skills to check out the client's understanding of what each of these skills means. The placing of the client's and the practitioner's initials on the diagnostic chart is a simple behavioral step to symbolize and observably confirm their joint understanding. Skill behaviors that the client cannot initial may remain on the chart; but the lack of the client's initials indicates that these skill behaviors must be reexplored before treatment programs for these behaviors are implemented. Only in the case of very low-level functioning clients, who must be placed in a rehabilitation treatment program irrespective of their own comprehension, does it make sense to institute such a program without prior client approval and understanding. In such instances as these, the practitioner may want to work with significant others to help implement the treatment program. An important principle to remember is that rehabilitation outcome is practically impossible without client involvement and understanding of the diagnostic plan; thus, the entire diagnostic interviewing and planning process is designed to maximize the input and understanding of the psychiatrically disabled client.

The review process itself often stimulates the discovery of other relevant skill areas that have not been identified previously. Sometimes the review process unexpectedly triggers an insight about a skill behavior that had heretofore gone unmentioned. During the review process, the practitioner may wish to take the time to deliberately expand the diagnostic chart in order to ensure that the diagnosis has in fact been comprehensive. This may be especially important if the practitioner is planning on referring the client to other treatment programs.

One way in which the list of diagnosed strengths and deficits can be comprehensively expanded is by determining if a client skill that has been categorized in one environmental area is also critical in another skill area. This expansion process is essentially a structured information-seeking interview. The rehabilitation practitioner simply checks whether each strength or deficit that has been diagnosed as critical in one environmental area might not also help or hamper the client's rehabilitative functioning in a different environmental area. The practitioner accomplishes this by first focusing on each individual skill within the living environment and asking the client, *"Will this behavior also help (interfere) with your success in (school) (work)?"* If yes, the practitioner also places that skill behavior on the client diagnostic chart in the new environmental area, then reviews with the client their mutual understanding of the skill behavior and confirms their understanding by initialing the new behavior. If the client and practitioner believe that the skill is relevant to other areas, the practitioner and client focus on the next skill in that area and repeat the questioning procedure for each skill behavior in the living environment. Then they repeat the entire procedure in the learning and/or working environments.

By conducting this information-seeking interview, the rehabilitation practitioner will begin to discern certain deficit patterns in the client's functioning as well as certain areas of client strength. For example, in the working area the client may have a deficit in terms of punctuality skills (i.e., the client's past behavior indicates that he or she has been routinely late in getting to work), but in the living area the client is always on time for church and recreational activities. Data such as this will give the practitioner information relevant to the eventual treatment plan. That is, a specific skill behavior that cannot be performed in one environment but can be performed in another environment may suggest a different type of rehabilitation treatment program than that needed for a deficit behavior that limits functioning in more than one environmental area. In the first instance, the client can actually perform the skill; he or she must simply learn to *apply* the skill in certain environments. In the second instance, the client cannot perform the skill in any environment; he or she must learn or *acquire* the skill. Thus, after the expansion process has been completed, the unique pattern of strengths and deficits that emerges will give clues to the environmental area in which the client is strongest and how specific or general certain strengths and deficit behaviors are.

At this particular time in the diagnostic planning process, the client or the practitioner may also want to suggest additional strengths and deficits that the client has not yet considered. An awareness of other critical skill behaviors is often stimulated by the review process. If the client and practitioner understand what is meant by these behaviors and agree that they are critical, those new behaviors can be added to the chart and initialed. It would now be appropriate — particularly for the client who seems overwhelmed by the diagnosis of a number of deficits — to deliberately suggest some client strengths. Some clients definitely need to be encouraged to expand their assets and strengths; these clients are often blinded to their assets by an unhealthy preoccupation with their deficits.

Table 21 depicts a psychiatrically disabled client's diagnostic chart after the expanding process has been completed. The client is an inpatient who will probably be discharged to a halfway house and day hospital. The behaviors in parentheses are those added during the expanding process, either by expanding the same behavior to other environmental areas or by direct suggestion by the rehabilitation practitioner.

Table 21.
A Completed Diagnostic Planning Chart

CLIENT DIAGNOSTIC PLANNING CHART   Name: R.C.

Situational Problems: Being discharged from inpatient ward.

Rehabilitation Goals: Arrange to live in a halfway house.

Environment	Strengths / Deficits	Physical Skills	Emotional Skills	Intellectual Skills
Living				
Halfway House (evenings)	+	Personal grooming skills. *RC WA* (Housework) *RC WA*	Converse with roommates. *RC WA* (Control temper) *RC WA*	Assist in kitchen *RC WA* Following a daily schedule. *RC WA*
Day Hospital Care	−	Travel to day hospital. *RC WA* Waking up in morning. *RC WA* Staying awake during day. *RC WA*	Speaking during house meeting. *RC WA* Participating in day-care group activities. *RC WA*	(Setting goals for self). *RC WA* (Reinforcing self). *RC WA*
Learning				
Adult Education	+	Attend to instructor. *RC WA*	Listen to instructor. *RC WA*	Remember class assignments. *RC WA*
Class at Halfway House	−	Sit through entire class. *RC WA*	(Converse with classmates or instructor). *RC WA*	Perform simple computation. *RC WA*
Working				
Not Applicable at Present	+ −			

106

Practice Situations

You can practice to improve your own reviewing skills by using the information provided in the Diagnostic Planning Chart developed in Table 21. Use a colleague knowledgeable in rehabilitation diagnostic planning skills to role-play this client. Lead into your review by first introducing the process and then illustrating what is involved with an explain-demonstrate-practice example. Conduct the expanding part of the review by asking whether or not deficits may exist in more than one environmental area. Do this expansion process for each environmental area. Any additional skill areas that you and the client discover can also be added to the chart. If possible, tape record the interaction and evaluate whether an understanding of each skill behavior was achieved. Have a colleague also evaluate how well he or she can understand what is meant by each skill. Repeat this process until you are able to use your reviewing skills without confusion or hesitation.

Once you are accomplished in the practice sessions, attempt the review process with a client with whom you are presently working. Remember that the objective of the review process is to increase the probability that your diagnostic plan is understandable and comprehensive. The value of comprehensiveness is lessened if the client does not understand or agree with the new skill behaviors that have been added. The rehabilitation practitioner may therefore use her or his responding skills constantly to both check and improve the client's understanding of the added skill behaviors.

The completion of the Client Diagnostic Planning Chart (as in Table 21) is the final step of the understanding phase of the diagnostic planning process. The practitioner's use of various personalizing and categorizing skills has resulted in a comprehensive picture of the client's rehabilitation functioning, organized in such a way as to maximize client understanding. The next major stage of the diagnostic planning process is to observably and objectively *assess* the client's level of functioning in each of these skills areas.

CATEGORIZING THE CLIENT'S STRENGTHS AND DEFICITS: A SUMMARY

Goal: To portray the client's unique pattern of identified strengths and deficits in a way that maximizes diagnostic understanding and comprehensiveness.

1. Begin to personalize the client's specific strengths and weaknesses.

2. Show and explain to the client the Diagnostic Planning Chart (or some modification of the chart).

3. Categorize the client's strengths and weaknesses by skill and environmental areas.

4. Review with the client each diagnosed skill behavior and jointly initial those behaviors that are understandable to the client.

5. Expand the diagnosis by checking to determine if diagnosed strengths and deficits are relevant in more than one environmental area.

6. Expand the diagnosis by suggesting additional strengths and deficits that have been stimulated by the review process.

7. Review with the client those newly diagnosed skill behaviors and jointly initial those behaviors that are understandable to the client.

UNDERSTANDING: A SKILLED APPROACH

Face sagging with dejection and concern, Ben looked much older than his fifty years. "See, I know I'm okay now. I mean, I know I can't ever go back to drinking. But I can live with that. The thing is, though, that no one else is going to be all that sure about me."

"So you feel worried because the other people may not have the confidence in you that you have in yourself." Maria watched Ben closely as she responded once again to his feelings and the external reasons for these feelings.

"Yeah...and — well, I really want to get along good with people this time. When — when I started drinking before, it was always because I was on the outs with people. My wife. Or my kids. Or my boss. Whoever was around. I don't want them hanging over me worrying about whether I'm really straightened out or not."

Again Maria responded. "You feel pretty confident about licking your drinking thing. But you're afraid other people won't be able to accept you on your own terms."

Ben nodded. "Uh huh. I just really want them to accept me and respect me and not think about the past."

Now Maria was able to begin personalizing her responses to Ben. She knew that it was critically important for him to recognize and accept the extent of his own role in the situation. "You feel nervous about getting back into things because you're really not sure where you stand in other people's eyes."

Once again Maria's response was accurate. Ben looked at her and nodded. "Yeah, that's it in a nutshell. I just don't know where I stand. I want to be a good husband and father and — and employee or whatever. But they may all just see me as an ex-lush who can't be given too much responsibility. I've tried to think about ways I can get through to them, but in the end I always end up feeling down."

"It's really depressing when you can't figure out how to convince people you care about that you're really not going to drink any more." Here Maria framed a careful response that personalized Ben's problem

for him. She did not confront him. She did not put words in his mouth. Instead, she heard what he was really saying, what he was really meaning, and played it back to him in terms he could understand — and terms that, most importantly, put Ben himself in control of the problem.

Nor did Maria stop there. She went on to help Ben come to terms with other problems in different areas. With physical problems like Ben's poor diet and lack of exercise. With emotional problems like Ben's inability to tell people what he was really feeling. With intellectual problems like Ben's difficulty in planning each day's activities. Problems in every area of Ben's living, learning, and working life.

Maria took it slowly, making sure that she personalized each deficit and responded to Ben's reaction at every step. She went through the same process for each of Ben's strengths. And because much of the initial material that Maria was presenting stemmed from Ben's own statements, his own exploration, Ben himself was able to follow and understand and accept everything.

"It's funny," he said at one point, his expression far more relaxed than it had been earlier. "I feel like I'm seeing me for the first time. And it really is me — this is really who I am. And these are the things I've really got to do!" He grinned. "It's like starting at the bottom. The best thing is that you know you're headed up!"

Chapter 4 ASSESSING THE CLIENT'S PERSONAL STRENGTHS AND DEFICITS ▪

ASSESSING: AN UNSKILLED APPROACH

During their last several sessions, Ellen had helped Barbara to explore and organize a whole list of specific strengths and deficits relevant to her living environment. Barbara would have to deal with each of these skill behaviors as soon as she was ready to leave the hospital and resume her regular life.

"I guess my biggest problem is with my family," Barbara said. "I just couldn't seem to get along with them when I was at home. Jim always had to have everything just right — dinner ready when he came home, everything just where it was supposed to be. The kids were always racing around. They never listened to a word I said. And Jim's mother — listen, either she and I wouldn't talk at all or we'd end up arguing about the dumbest things. Like how long soft-boiled eggs are supposed to cook, for God's sake!" Barbara sighed. "If I could just keep things on an even keel with my family, I know I could work out all the other things we've talked about."

"You're right," Ellen told her. "I think developing a really good relationship with all the people in your family has got to be a major goal."

They spent the remainder of that session talking about different aspects of Barbara's present relationship with her family. Her two boys were ten and twelve, ages where they had far more energy and enthusiasm than self-control. Jim, Barbara's husband, was a hard-working guy but one who had trouble recognizing other people's needs. Barbara described how he had often yelled at her until she broke down and wept over some simple affair like weak coffee or a newspaper that had been left out in the rain instead of brought inside. Then there was old Mrs. Thompson, Jim's mother. Apparently she saw Barbara's most recent hospitalization as proof positive that her son had made a bad mistake when he married. Even now, Barbara's voice trembled when she talked about her relationship with the older woman.

The next session followed much the same pattern — and so did the one after that. Ellen worked with Barbara to try to pin down the problems that existed in her relationship with her family. She told Barbara that she must exercise firmer control over her children: "Tell them just what you expect of them and then make them stick to it." She encouraged Barbara to talk out her problems with Jim: "Just sit down with him and tell him how you get upset sometimes when he gets angry with you. He probably doesn't even realize how you feel..." She outlined vague strategies of dealing with Jim's mother: "Try to get her in-

111

volved in activities outside the house that she might enjoy — anything to get her out of your hair!"

Everything that Ellen said was well-intentioned. Some of it was even mildly constructive. Yet despite this, Barbara found it harder and harder to grab hold of any particular strategy or course of action. She knew she had to work to develop better relationships within her family. But she still could not see how she was supposed to do this. Most important, she did not have any clear idea of just what a "good relationship" was. How, then, was she supposed to know exactly what to do or whether or not she was getting closer to her goal?

The longer her sessions with Ellen dragged on, the worse Barbara seemed to feel. Each day brought her closer to the time when she would be home again — and yet she did not feel any closer to a solution to her major concern. What was she supposed to do? How would she know when she had done it?

For her part, Ellen suspected that things were not going so well as they might. The big shock, however, came the morning that Barbara failed to show up for her regular session. Ellen called the ward and learned that Barbara was asleep.

"We had to give her extra medication," Ellen was told. "She got pretty uptight last night — running around and upsetting everyone, including herself. I'm afraid it may be a few days before she's ready to start working with you again."

Now it was Ellen's turn to worry. Where had she gone wrong? Everything had gone so well right up to the last minute. Barbara had agreed that working for a better family relationship had to be a major goal. What had gone wrong?

*What had gone wrong, of course, was that the "goal" that Ellen had developed was actually not a goal at all but merely a vague direction. If a client is to work toward and achieve a goal, he or she must have a clear understanding of the specific, concrete things that the goal involves. When the goal is achieved, what will the client be **doing** or be able to do? What will others be **doing?***

A goal is a target. The less clear, tangible, and concrete it is, the greater the chance that the client will never achieve or "hit" it. Given the vague, general quality of the "goal" that Ellen developed, Barbara had no chance at all!

Once the client's deficits have been categorized PEI x LLW and then reviewed within these categories to ensure comprehensiveness and understandability, the final task of the diagnostic planning stage is to accurately *assess* exactly what is meant by each skill behavior.

The assessment stage of the diagnostic process essentially consists of three steps. In the first assessment step, *the practitioner writes a statement that operationalizes each skill behavior.* In this statement, the practitioner identifies in specific, observable terms the exact skill that needs to be performed. Next, *the practitioner quantifies the psychiatrically disabled client's present level of performance* for each skilled behavior. Lastly, *the practitioner quantifies the level of skilled performance the client will need* to function adequately in his or her environment. For identified strength areas, the present level will equal or exceed the needed level. For identified deficit areas, the present level will be less than the needed level. Once the practitioner has performed these steps, the discrepancies that exist between the client's present and needed levels of functioning in his or her deficit areas become the programmatic goals for the rehabilitation client.

One major difficulty that rehabilitation practitioners sometimes have during the assessment process is disciplining themselves to take the time to perform all three assessment steps. The temptation is strong to breeze through these assessment steps in the interests of efficiency. However, the efficiency and time gained are usually sacrificed in later phases of the rehabilitation treatment process. Consider the following two examples.

"LOOKING EFFICIENT"

Bob Johnson was a therapist in a large community mental health center. Many demands were placed on his time, foremost of which was his rather heavy caseload. As a result, Bob's assessment skills were rather slipshod. As assessment was a rather time-consuming process, Bob decided to cut some corners in this area and never really operationalized the client's strengths and deficits. Rather, Bob would consider the rehabilitation diagnostic plan complete when he and the client had identified strengths and deficits in certain environmental areas.

Thus, Bob Johnson's clients were started on their rehabilitation treatment programs when they had identified such deficits as, for example, lack of self-control in the living area and lack of job-interviewing skills in the working area. Unfortunately, Bob's inability to operationalize such client deficits set the stage for several problems in later phases of the rehabilitation treatment process. For example, when Bob attempted to develop systematic treatment programs he found that, without an observable goal, it became difficult to sequence some of the steps to the goal accurately. Difficulties also occurred when he tried to explain the client's goals to significant others in the client's life, as the concept of "self-control" meant different things to different people. Understandably, his clients had difficulty staying goal-directed when the goal was so abstract. Worst of all, when it came time to evaluate the outcome for each of his clients, it was very difficult to really know if his clients had actually reached their goals.

For Bob Johnson and his clients, cutting corners in the assessment phases of the diagnostic planning process led to later difficulties that, *in the long run, consumed more time than was saved by eliminating the assessment steps. Never really knowing **exactly** what the client needed to overcome helped create more problems than it solved.*

Compare Bob Johnson's attempts, which "look efficient," to Ruth Griffin's attempt to "be efficient."

"BEING EFFICIENT"

Ruth was always looking for places to cut corners. As a rehabilitation practitioner in a large community mental health center, she saw many clients each day. She was always looking for ways to do things more efficiently, but she knew that taking shortcuts in the assessment phase would only backfire.

Thus, she made sure that, before any rehabilitation programming occurred, both she and the client knew exactly the client's present and needed levels of functioning for each skill area. For example, a given deficit was not just categorized as a "lack of self-control in the living area," but was observably assessed as "client presently raises voice to spouse five times a week during mealtime conversations and needs to reduce the frequency to zero times per week."

By assessing her clients in such an observable, measurable way, several advantages immediately accrued to Ruth and her clients. First, systematic rehabilitation programs could be more easily developed when the program goals were so observable. Second, significant others in the clients' lives knew exactly what the treatment programs were trying to accomplish. Third, Ruth's clients themselves could become more involved in the treatment program when the goals were less esoteric and more understandable. And fourth, the rehabilitation outcome of each client could be specifically assessed so that specific types of treatment intervention programs could be evaluated and improved.

Ruth, by using all her assessment skills, was in actuality cutting corners. By observably measuring each skill deficit, she was more effective in her program development, more efficient in explaining the rehabilitation goals to her clients and significant others, and more equipped to eventually evaluate the rehabilitation outcome of her clients.

OPERATIONALIZING EACH IMPORTANT SKILL BEHAVIOR

Before the actual process of quantifying or measuring skilled behaviors can occur, *the rehabilitation practitioner determines exactly what behavior is going to be quantified.* Specifically, this procedure involves operationalizing the skill, that is, writing an assessment statement that indicates: *who* is performing the behavior; *what* skill behavior the person is performing; *how* the behavior is to be measured; *what* the observable behavioral components are; and *when* and/or *where* the observable behavior is to be performed. By indicating these specific details for each identified skill, the rehabilitation practitioner has defined exactly what this skilled behavior means *for this particular client*. If practitioners skip this important step of operationalizing those specific behaviors that might become the goals of rehabilitation treatment, the field of rehabilitation will be replicating the same problem that has plagued the defenders of the field of psychotherapy: an historical inability to document the effectiveness of psychotherapeutic treatment.

One of the reasons the continual challenges to the efficacy of counseling and psychotherapy (Eysenck, 1952, 1960, 1972) cannot be completely answered is that therapists have typically not defined their goals in observable terms. For example, therapists often describe clients as needing to become more "motivated, adjusted, self-actualized, self-accepting, congruent, insightful" and so on. These goals certainly do not describe an observable activity; as a result, their attainment by clients would be difficult to document and verify. Thus, even if therapy were having a positive impact on its clients, the adherents of psychotherapy would still be unable to demonstrate the capabilities of their methods without first defining their goals in observable terms. The critics of psychotherapy have not claimed that psychotherapy is *ineffective;* rather, they have pointed out that the existing evidence has failed to indicate that psychotherapy *is effective* (Eysenck, 1972). In other words, the burden of proof is on the provider of the service; and until therapeutic goals are defined in a more observable and meaningful manner, therapeutic effectiveness will be difficult to document. In contrast, the rehabilitation practitioner, by assessing the areas of rehabilitation concern in an observable and objective manner, can ensure that the groundwork has been laid for a meaningful evaluation of the client's rehabilitation outcome.

In addition, there is evidence to suggest that making observable assessments of client goals has a motivating effect on the client's and/or the helper's performance. Perhaps one of the most intriguing findings with respect to assessment is that simply requiring the therapist to set observable goals seems to improve therapeutic outcome in and of itself. In an experimental study of the benefits of goal assessment, Smith (1976) had one group of adolescent clients counseled by professional therapists in their own style with one notable exception: The therapists had been instructed in how to set observable goals for their clients. Another group of therapists counseled their clients without receiving prior training in defining observable client goals. At the end of eight counseling sessions, the group of clients aided by counselors who had defined observable goals showed significantly greater improvement on a variety of counseling outcome indices.

Walker (1972) has studied the importance of assessment based on his interest in developing evaluative procedures within the helping professions. In studying an agency designed to rehabilitate the hard-core unemployed, Walker found that when feedback to practitioners about how well their clients were achieving observable rehabilitation goals was experimentally withdrawn, the number of clients rehabilitated decreased; likewise, when the practitioners were once again provided with feedback as to how well their clients were achieving their goals, the rehabilitation outcome improved once again. In other words, the assessment of observable client goals combined with feedback to the practitioners in terms of how well the clients are achieving these goals can, in and of itself, improve an agency's rehabilitation outcome.

Besides this empirical evidence related to the value of making observable assessments, there are also some programmatic reasons. The same skill activity is typically defined in different ways for different clients, depending on the nature of each client's exploration of that particular skill behavior. The need for writing assessment statements in such detail is, in part, a function of this fact — that the same skill area can mean two different things to two different clients and, thus, must be defined very specifically to ensure relevance to each client's unique situation.

For example, two different housewives may each have identified a deficit that has been categorized in the emotional-living area — an inability to discipline their children. This deficit is one of several preventing each of these women from resuming her role as head of the household. This deficit has been categorized on the Client Diagnostic Planning Chart as a deficit in "disciplining children." However, although these deficit statements appear the same on the Diagnostic Planning Chart, in reality the assessment statement written for each of these women may vary tremendously as a function of the unique situation in which each finds herself. Thus, for Mrs. Jones, the rehabilitation practitioner may operationalize the following assessment statement:

"Mrs. Jones cannot discipline her children as measured by the frequency of noncorporal discipline methods she uses each week at home when her husband is not present."

In contrast, for Mrs. Smith, the rehabilitation practitioner may write the following assessment statement:

"Mrs. Smith cannot discipline her children as measured by the amount of time it takes her to send a misbehaving child to a time-out room when the child is misbehaving in front of company.

The previous two assessment statements are clearly for two different people who have experienced different kinds of trouble in disciplining their children. The assessment statement is written for a discipline problem that manifests itself in two entirely different ways. The exact phrasing of the assessment statement depends on how each client presents the strength or deficit and is a function of that client's and the practitioner's understanding of the client's unique situation. These two assessment statements contain the essential components that ensure specificity and observability:

Who:	Mrs. Jones	Mrs. Smith
What Skill:	Discipline children	Discipline children
How Measured:	The frequency per week.	Amount of time it takes.
What Behavior:	Use noncorporal discipline methods.	Send misbehaving child to time-out room.
When/Where:	At home when husband is not present.	When company is present.

Specifically, the identification of *who* is performing the skill and *what* the skill is called had already been done when the skill was placed on the Diagnostic Planning Chart. A skill categorized on the Client Diagnostic Planning Chart indicates that the *who* is the client. Thus, although the information regarding "who" has been noted already, it should be pointed out that errors may sometimes occur in this process. For example, an assessment statement of a client skill should not begin:
"The practitioner talks to the client..."

In this example, the practitioner has been incorrectly identified as the person who must perform the skill behavior. Although the rehabilitation *program* that is developed may eventually contain steps that involve the practitioner "telling the client," this is not a proper rehabilitation assessment statement. If it were, the rehabilitation outcome could be achieved by the client merely being the passive recipient rather than an active participant.

Another common error occurs when an inanimate object is identified as having the skill, as in the beginning of this assessment statement:
"The work setting can be modified..."

Once again, the client has *not* been identified as having the skill deficit. Although the rehabilitation treatment program that is developed may have a step in it that involves modifying the work setting, this is not an appropriate rehabilitation assessment statement since it relegates the client to a passive role in the rehabilitation program.

Once the person and the particular skill the person is performing have been identified from the Client Diagnostic Planning Chart, the next two steps involve specifying *how* the skill behavior will be measured and *what* observable behavior will be measured. In specifying exactly what the observable behavior is, practitioners often experience difficulty because so many of the words commonly used in mental health settings do not describe an observable action or a product of an observable action. For example, mental health professionals often refer to their clients as needing to become more motivated, responsible, mature, and congruent; or, needing to develop a stronger self-concept, more ego strength, and a better self-identity. Although these terms may have meaning to mental health professionals, they do not depict specific, measurable, observable activities. In order to write a rehabilitation assessment statement, the rehabilitation practitioner must employ a vocabulary that describes behavior capable of being observed and measured. Thus, descriptive words such as *earn, spend, work, attend, say, operate, write, list,* and *reside* are capable of describing what a client can or cannot do in terms specific enough so that witnesses to the client's actions could agree on whether the activity had occurred or not. Words such as *demonstrate, perform,* and *exhibit* followed by an observable action are also useful in writing a rehabilitation assessment statement. The key to describing a client behavior in observable terms is to ask yourself, "Can I and others experience either that behavior or the product of that behavior with at least one of our five senses?" (Obviously, most client behaviors are considered observable because these behaviors can be seen and/or heard.)

If the answer to the question about observability is affirmative, the practitioner can then determine *how* the observable behavior will be measured. Behaviors are typically measured in terms of time, frequency, or amount. For example:

Time: *Amount of time* client takes to walk one mile

Frequency: *Number of times per week* the client gets to sleep by midnight

Amount: *Amount of money* client earns working

Once these behaviors are described observably and in a manner that will allow them to be measured or quantified, the practitioner can ensure that the skill behavior is specific enough by determining whether this behavior is to be performed at any special time or place (*when* or *where*). It is important to qualify each observable behavior in this way in order to ensure situational specificity. In this way, any special conditions under which the client is doing the skilled behavior can be sufficiently described. For example, the behavior of "working" may vary with respect to *when* a client is working (e.g., part-time, full-time) or *where* a client is working (e.g. sheltered workshop, sheltered employment, competitive employment). Other examples are:

Where: Amount of time client takes to walk the one mile *from his/her home to the day hospital*

When: Number of times per week client gets to sleep by midnight *on nights before a working day*

When/Where: Amount of money client earns working *part-time in a competitive employment setting*

Table 22 is an example of assessment statements written for all the skill behaviors previously categorized in Table 21 in Chapter 3. The *who* is indicated at the top of the assessment chart and *what* PEI skill activity is indicated in the left-hand margin. *How* the observable behavior is being measured and *what* the observable behavior actually is are stated in the wide middle column. In addition, any special conditions with respect to *when* and *where* are also included in this column. Note that whether the behavior was initially considered to be a strength or deficit is indicated by the pluses and minuses in the third column. The final two columns, which are blank for now, will be filled in during the next two steps of the assessment stage. As usual, the specific living, learning, and working environments under consideration are indicated.

Practice Situations

After examining Table 22 and the unique manner in which each skill activity is defined, try to write a different assessment statement for each skill activity. In particular, try to modify *how* the behavior is defined observably and *when* or *where* it can be measured. Just as we took the skill of disciplining children and wrote two very different assessment statements, you can practice operationalizing assessment statements by reassessing the skill activities of Table 22. Write your assessment statements in the Client Assessment Chart illustrated in Table 23.

Another way to improve your ability to write operationalized assessment statements is to practice on those skill activities that you developed for yourself in Table 17 in Chapter 3. Try to write assessment statements on a Client Assessment Chart so that the way in which you actually assess these behaviors has meaning to your own unique life experience. Operationalize at least five physical, five emotional, and five intellectual skill behaviors.

Based on these practice attempts, it should now be clear that some skill areas lend themselves more easily to writing observable assessment statements. In particular, the client's physical area of functioning is often the easiest category within which to write observable assessment statements. This is no doubt because the categorization of a behavior as physical involves a physical act of some type that often has the measuring device "built into" the behavior (e.g., walking a certain distance; sleeping for a certain time; lifting a certain weight). In contrast, the skills in the emotional area are typically the most difficult to make observable and measurable. Make sure in your practice attempts that you have sufficiently tested your assessment skills in the emotional area of functioning.

As you become increasingly proficient in writing operationalized assessment statements, begin to write rehabilitation assessment statements for clients for whom you have already developed a Diagnostic Planning Chart. Remember that one of the principles of rehabilitation diagnostic planning is to involve the client in the process to the greatest extent possible.

Table 22.

Sample Client Assessment Chart Showing Operationalized Skill Activities

CLIENT ASSESSMENT CHART

Name _____

Situational Problem: Being discharged from inpatient ward.

_____

_____

Rehabilitation Goal: To arrange to live in a halfway house.

_____

_____

PEI Skill Activity	+	Skill Behavior	Level of Functioning	
	−		Present	Needed
Living Environment Goal: Halfway house (evenings and night); day hospital (days)				
P Grooming	+	Number of days per week client can dress and wash self at a level rated as "Acceptable" by day hospital supervisor.		
P Housework	+	Number of room-cleaning behaviors client performs each day from list of 3 appropriate room-cleaning behaviors (make bed, sweep floor, pick up clothes).		
P Traveling	−	Amount of time client takes to travel from halfway house to day hospital.		

PEI Skill Activity	+/-	Skill Behavior	Level of Functioning Present	Needed
Living Environment Goal: Halfway house (evenings and night); day hospital (days)				
E Conversations	+ / -	Number of interactions lasting 30 seconds or more client performs with people with whom he is living.		
E Controlling Temper	+	Number of crying-yelling outbursts per week client exhibits during evening and night.		
E Speaking Up	–	Number of times per meeting client can speak about self or environment in halfway house or day hospital without being called upon.		
I Kitchen Assisting	+	Percent of time it takes client to perform certain kitchen task in relation to the time it typically takes other clients.		
I Scheduling	+	Percent of daily scheduled activities that client accomplishes on time without prompting by staff.		
I Setting Goals	–	Number of weekly goals client lists for self.		
I Reinforcing	–	Percent of time client rewards or punishes self based on his/her ability to achieve goals set for self.		
Learning Environment Goal: Adult Education Class at halfway house				
I Paying Attention	+	Percent of time client looks directly at instructor when instructor is speaking.		
E Listening	+	Percent of time client can repeat main points of instructor's presentation when called upon.		
E Conversation	–	Number of times client talks (one second or more) with either instructor or classmates during class session.		
Working Environment: Not applicable at present				

121

Table 23.

Practice Client Assessment Chart for Operationalizing Skill Activity

CLIENT ASSESSMENT CHART

Name _____

Situational Problem: _____

Rehabilitation Goal: _____

PEI	Skill Activity	+	−	Skill Behavior	Level of Functioning	
					Present	Needed
	Living Environment:					
	Learning Environment:					
	Working Environment:					

Although most clients do not have the ability to write assessment statements, the client's input is needed so that the statements created are unique to the client's specific skill behaviors. Thus, the practitioner must attempt to check out with the client each diagnostic statement as it is developed.

OPERATIONALIZING SKILL BEHAVIORS: A SUMMARY

Goal: To define the client's previously diagnosed skills in the most behavioral, observable terms possible.

1. Indicate *who* is performing the behavior.
2. Indicate *what* skill behavior is being performed.
3. Indicate *how* the behavior is being measured.
4. Indicate *what* the observable behavioral components are.
5. Indicate *when* and/or *where* the observable behavior is being performed.

QUANTIFYING THE CLIENT'S PRESENT LEVEL OF SKILL FUNCTIONING

Now that the operationalized assessment statement has defined observable skill behaviors in detail and has indicated how these behaviors will be measured, *the next step is to assess the client's present level of functioning for each skill behavior.* This measurement is an important step in the entire rehabilitation process. It is difficult to develop an efficient treatment program if the client's present level of functioning has not been specifically ascertained. The first step of the rehabilitation treatment program is geared to each individual client's present capabilities. In addition, the later steps in the rehabilitation program are a function of where the client begins the program. A rough analogy would be that of a car trip: The type of trip that is planned is a function of whether the beginning point of the trip is in Alaska or Florida. In essence, the point of departure — whether it be a trip or a treatment program — has implications for the plan that emerges. In addition, it is critical to know the client's present level of functioning so that the practitioner can ascertain the *degree* of client deficit for each particular skill behavior or determine if, in fact, a deficit really does exist. Obviously the degree of deficit cannot be determined until the skill demands of the environment are also quantified and then compared with the client's present level of functioning in that particular skill.

It must be pointed out that the client's skills do not *have* to be quantified exactly in order for a rehabilitation treatment program to be im-

123

plemented. For example, a treatment program can be initiated based on the operationalized assessment statement that the client lacks "leisure-time skills" — that is, "participates very rarely in recreational activities with family." In this situation there is no numerical indication of the exact number of activities in which the client presently engages, nor needs to engage. However, this limited degree of measurement still allows for the implementation of a treatment program designed to *increase* the client's leisure-time skills. The only absolute requirement is that the skill behavior be described in an observable manner, that is, operationalized. At a minimum, the practitioner defines *who* is performing the skill, *what* behavior is being performed, *when* and/or *where* it is performed. It is possible to develop a treatment program capable of improving the client's skills without quantifying *how well* the client is presently performing the skill or needs to perform the skill. It is sometimes enough to know that the client's behavior is deficient and needs to improve.

An example of how it is *not* always necessary to quantify the skill in order to improve it can be provided by the sporting world. Suppose a tennis player wants to improve her ability to get her first serve into the service court. It would be possible to develop a program to improve her tennis service without quantifying her present and needed level of functioning (for example, present level = 30 percent of first serves in service court; needed level = 60 percent of first serves in service court). A program can be successfully implemented knowing only that her serving ability is deficient and that she wants to improve.

Thus, it is possible to improve skills without quantification, as long as the behavior is operationalized. This lack of quantification can be the preferred situation in instances where the client or significant other resists the measurement process. This resistance may be due to feelings that the assigning of numbers is too "mechanistic" or "makes me feel like a number." Other times, the client might resent being "pinned down" as to his or her present or needed level of functioning. In such cases, the practitioner can try to discuss the problem or simply drop the measurement phrase of the operationalized statement. For example, the skill deficit of "reinforcing," which was operationalized as "the percent of times the client regards or punishes self based on client's ability to achieve goals for self," can be redefined as "the client's ability to reward or punish self based on the client's ability to achieve goals for self needs to be *improved*."

Table 24 presents the skills previously defined in Table 22 quantified in terms of the client's present level of functioning. Note that the only additions in the Client Assessment Chart are the numbers in the column under "Present Level." Each of these numbers is understandable by referring to the corresponding assessment statement. For example, the client can dress and wash self at a level rated as "Acceptable" by the day-hospital supervisor 7 days a week, and the client can perform 2 room-cleaning behaviors each day.

The methods by which the numbers were arrived at vary considerably. Much of the available information was developed previously in the diagnostic planning process. That is, while the practitioner and the client were exploring, understanding, and writing assessment statements, information was constantly being developed from which measurements could be estimated quite accurately by the practitioner. For example, through the practitioner's interactions with the client and discussion of the skills of setting goals and reinforcing self, the practitioner and client realized that the client *never* engages in such behavior.

Another method of collecting the information from which to quantify the client's present level of functioning is simply to ask the client to estimate in numerical terms her or his present level of functioning. Although clients cannot do this for all skill behaviors, and although some clients cannot do this for any skill behaviors, many clients are quite capable of accurately estimating their own performance.

Indeed, the extent to which the client has been involved in the diagnostic planning process and comprehends the assessment statements is a rough indicator of how helpful the client can be in making estimates of her or his present functioning. The client illustrated in Table 24, for example, was able to estimate the number of times he loses his temper per week as well as his ability to travel from the halfway house to the day hospital.

The final two methods of collecting information relevant to quantifying the client's present level of functioning can also serve as a check of the accuracy of any existing assessment. These two methods involve either setting up a testing situation in which the client's skill behavior can be observed and/or by asking significant others in the client's life to estimate the client's present functioning. Significant others in the client's life would include such people as relatives, friends, employers, teachers, and treatment personnel. The practitioner can simply read to the significant other the rehabilitation assessment statement in question and ask him or her to estimate the client's present ability. The fact that the assessment statement has been written in specific, observable terms greatly facilitates this process. At this time the practitioner can also use the input of significant others to check the accuracy of estimates made by the client and practitioner but about which the latter still feels doubtful.

Some examples from Table 24 are: grooming was rated by a ward nurse; housework by his mother; paying attention and listening were estimated by the client and corroborated by the hospital workshop director.

As suggested above, the final method used to quantify the client's present level of functioning involves setting up a testing situation that provides the client the opportunity to demonstrate his or her present level of functioning. The advantage of a testing method (particularly role-playing, simulation, or real-life observation) is that it gives the

125

Table 24.

Sample Client Assessment Chart Showing Present Level of Functioning

CLIENT ASSESSMENT CHART

Name _____

Situational Problem: Being discharged from inpatient ward.

Rehabilitation Goal: To arrange to live in a halfway house.

PEI	Skill Activity	+/−	Skill Behavior	Level of Functioning	
				Present	Needed
Living Environment: Goal: Halfway house (evenings and nights); day hospital (days)					
P	Grooming	+	Number of days per week client can dress and wash self at a level rated as "Acceptable" by day-hospital supervisor.	7	
P	Housework	+	Number of room-cleaning behaviors client performs each day from list of 3 appropriate room-cleaning behaviors (make bed, sweep floor, pick up clothes).	2	
P	Traveling	−	Amount of time client takes to travel from halfway house to day hospital.	Unable	
E	Conversations	+	Number of interactions lasting 30 seconds or more client performs with people with whom he is living.	20	
E	Controlling Temper	+	Number of crying-yelling outbursts per week client exhibits during evening and night.	1	

PEI	Skill Activity	+ –	Skill Behavior	Level of Functioning	
				Present	Needed
Living Environment: Goal: Halfway house (evenings and nights); day hospital (days)					
E	Speaking Up	–	Number of times per meeting client can speak about self or environment in halfway house or day hospital without being called upon.	0	
I	Kitchen Assisting	+	Percent of time it takes client to perform certain kitchen task in relation to the time it typically takes other clients.	150%	
I	Scheduling	+	Percent of daily scheduled activities that client accomplishes on time without prompting by staff.	100%	
I	Setting Goals	–	Number of weekly goals client lists for self.	0	
I	Reinforcing	–	Percent of time client rewards or punishes self based on his/her ability to achieve goals set for self.	0%	
Learning Environment: Adult Education Class at halfway house					
I	Paying Attention	+	Percent of time client looks directly at instructor when instructor is speaking.	50%	
E	Listening	+	Percent of time client can repeat main points of instructor's presentation when called upon.	50%	
E	Conversation	–	Number of times client talks (one second or more) with either instructor or classmates during class session.	0	
Working Environment: Not applicable at present					

practitioner an opportunity for first-hand observation and affords the client a direct experience of his or her present ability. The disadvantage with role-playing and simulation is that the situation is contrived and that the client's behavior may not approximate her or his functioning in the real-world situation. Nevertheless, such artificial testing situations do remain a viable method of obtaining data about a client's present level of functioning. In addition, these methods can be used as a check on the accuracy of information gathered from other sources. An example might be checking the client's estimate of his kitchen-assisting skills by setting up a kitchen-assisting task in the day-hospital kitchen.

If conflicting data is obtained and the practitioner cannot make any distinctions between the validity of these conflicting measurements, the most appropriate resolution is to use the lower estimate of the client's functioning. The rationale here is that there is more danger in beginning a rehabilitation program at too high a level than at too low a level. That is, if the client's ability is overestimated and a treatment program is developed which starts at this high level, the client will experience immediate failure. On the other hand, if the client's ability is underestimated and a treatment program is developed that starts at a low level, the client will still experience success. The rehabilitation practitioner in charge of the treatment program can then move the client quickly through those earlier steps until the client reaches that particular part of the program that is reflective of her or his present capabilities.

Practice Situations

Improve your ability to quantify the client's present level by using the assessment statements that you redefined from Table 22 to fill in a hypothetical Client Assessment Chart (similar to Table 22). Indicate on a separate sheet of paper your hypotheses as to what method you used to collect the information from which you quantified the client's present level. That is, do you think the information would have been: (1) already developed during the exploration and understanding process and estimated by the practitioner; (2) an estimate by the client; (3) an estimate by significant others; and/or (4) developed from a testing situation?

Use at least one testing example as a basis for gathering information about one hypothetical client skill behavior. Be prepared to describe the particulars of the testing situation in terms of how you would set it up. Also describe how you would use significant others or the testing method as a check of at least one behavior estimated by the client. In essence, this entire practice situation is a repeat of what was just done in the preceding pages using Table 22 as the hypothetical client.

Another way to practice the process of quantifying present levels of skilled behaviors is to take the assessment statements that you wrote on yourself and try to quantify your own present level of functioning. Check out your own measurements of your skill levels by reviewing some of your assessments with significant others and by setting up at least one testing situation.

Once you have practiced this skill on hypothetical clients and on yourself, begin to quantify the present abilities of a client with whom you have written assessment statements. Record these numbers on the Client Assessment Chart. As in all other stages of the assessment process, try to involve the client in the quantification process as much as possible. The actual measurement process provides the client with a simple yet strong dose of reality. The practitioner must be certain to observe the client's response to this process and, if necessary, explore with the client the importance of this new and more specific knowledge concerning the client's present abilities.

QUANTIFYING THE CLIENT'S PRESENT LEVEL OF FUNCTIONING: A SUMMARY

Goal: To estimate as exactly as possible the client's present level of functioning in diagnosed skill areas.

1. Operationalize the client's previously diagnosed skills.

2. Estimate the client's present level of functioning by using information previously collected during the diagnostic planning process;

   and/or

3. Obtain the client's estimate of his or her present functioning;

   and/or

4. Ask significant others to estimate client's present functioning;

   and/or

5. Set up a testing situation in which the client demonstrates his or her present level of functioning.

6. If conflicting estimates occur, use the lower estimate of the client's functioning.

QUANTIFYING THE CLIENT'S NEEDED LEVEL OF SKILL FUNCTIONING

Once the present level of client functioning has been quantified, *the next step is to quantify the client's level of physical, emotional, and intellectual functioning needed* to function adequately in his or her particular living, learning, and/or working environment. Like the quantification of the client's present level, the measurement of the client's needed level is an important step in the rehabilitation diagnostic process. In order to plan a rehabilitation treatment program efficiently, the practitioner must know what the program is trying to achieve. The analogy of the car trip still holds — your travel program will be very different depending on whether you are traveling from San Francisco to Los Angeles or from San Francisco to Boston. In essence, the final goal — whether it be a trip or a program — must be identified before the planning can be meaningfully carried out. Also, the client's needed level of functioning is critical to know so that, by comparing the needed level to present level, the practitioner has an excellent estimate of whether or not a skill is a strength or deficit and the *degree* of client skill deficit.

There are essentially two methods involved in quantifying the client's needed level of functioning. The first method involves measuring the client's needed level of functioning for those environments which the practitioner and client have identified as the most suitable for the client. The second method involves quantifying the client's needed levels of functioning for other possible environments. That is, the client is typically referred to a rehabilitation practitioner with a tentative environmental setting in mind; and the client's skill behaviors are typically explored and understood in relation to this tentative environmental setting. The tentative environment varies in terms of specificity (e.g., "sales clerk at Jones' Store" or "full-time competitive employment"). Unfortunately, in many cases no real choice of environment exists. Often the client is forced to live with her or his family because few other desirable possibilities are available and affordable. In terms of employment, a client's poor employment history and accompanying lack of job skills often preclude many jobs. Other factors determining the particular environment in which the client may function are the specific desires of the client and the client's significant others. A final influential factor is the initial judgment of the psychiatric treatment and rehabilitation practitioners as to the client's probability of succeeding in a particular environment. All of these factors contribute to the early identification of the client's tentative environmental settings.

During the assessment stage, however, there is an excellent opportunity for systematically considering alternatives to the tentative environmental settings identified earlier. At this time the client and practitioner can consider what level of functioning the client would need to achieve if he or she wished to function in other environments.

For example, a client who has been hospitalized recently due to severe problems in her living environment may tentatively identify her working environment as the same job in which she was previously employed. If she would also like to assess the level of functioning she would need in order to get a different position, however, this could be done during this step in the diagnostic planning process.

In Table 25 the needed level of functioning is quantified for those skills that were previously assessed in Table 22 and quantified in terms of present level in Table 24. Note that the only new additions to the Client Assessment Chart are the numbers in the column under "Needed Level." Each of these numbers is understandable by referring to the corresponding assessment statement. For example, the client needs to be able to use personal grooming skills 7 times per week, 3 room-cleaning behaviors per day, and travel in *30-40* minutes from the halfway house to the day hospital.

The critical dimension that must be assessed with respect to quantifying environmental settings is whether or not the client has the skills needed to be successful *in that environment*. The adult education class should certainly teach this client the skills to overcome other deficits. However, what is reflected on the Client Assessment Chart is, "Does the client have the ability to function in that particular environment?" — not, "What skills are lacking that make him need an adult education class?" For example, perhaps one of the deficits identified for the client in Table 22 is that he has no hobbies or activities. Although this behavior might be considered a deficit if the client were considering a return to his family setting, it may not be in a halfway house environment. If the goal of the halfway house is to return the client eventually to a home environment, however, this behavior may be considered a deficit and be treated by means of adult education classes at the halfway house.

At this stage in the diagnostic planning process, it is also appropriate to check to see that what were initially considered strengths are in fact strengths and that what were initially considered deficits are in fact deficits. In the example depicted in Tables 24 and 25, we see that the assessment process has indicated unanticipated deficits in the skills of housework and kitchen assisting.

The methods used to quantify the client's needed level of functioning are essentially the same methods used to quantify the client's present level of functioning, with the exception of the testing method. Thus, the practitioner can estimate the needed level of particular skills by drawing on information collected during the diagnostic planning process. For example, the rehabilitation practitioner might estimate that if the client in Table 25 is going to profit from the adult education class, he must be able to pay attention and listen a minimum of 50 percent of the time.

The client's own ability to estimate the level of functioning that she or he will need in a particular environment varies according to how familiar the client is with that environment. If the client will be returning to an environment in which she or he has functioned previously, the client will obviously have a better idea of what is needed than if the environment is an unfamiliar one. For example, if the client is returning home and to a former school or job, he or she will be in a better position to make estimates than if the rehabilitation plan involves the client's first attempt at residing in a day hospital or halfway house.

Table 25.
Sample Client Assessment Chart Showing Needed Level of Functioning

CLIENT ASSESSMENT CHART

Name _____

Situational Problem: Being discharged from inpatient ward.

Rehabilitation Goal: To arrange to live in a halfway house.

PEI	Skill Activity	+ –	Skill Behavior	Level of Functioning	
				Present	Needed
Living Environment: Goal: Halfway house (evenings and nights); day hospital (days)					
P	Grooming	+	Number of days per week client can dress and wash self at a level rated as "Acceptable" by day hospital supervisor.	7	7
P	Housework	+	Number of room-cleaning behaviors client performs each day from list of 3 appropriate room-cleaning behaviors (make bed, sweep floor, pick up clothes).	2	3
P	Traveling	–	Amount of time client takes to travel from halfway house to day hospital.	Unable	30'–40'
E	Conversations	+	Number of interactions lasting 30 seconds or more client performs with people with whom he is living.	20	10
E	Controlling Temper	+	Number of crying-yelling outbursts per week client exhibits during evening and night.	1	1

PEI	Skill Activity	+/-	Skill Behavior	Level of Functioning	
				Present	Needed

Living Environment: Goal: Halfway house (evenings and nights); day hospital (days)

PEI	Skill Activity	+/-	Skill Behavior	Present	Needed
E	Speaking Up	–	Number of times per meeting client can speak about self or environment in halfway house or day hospital without being called upon.	0	2
I	Kitchen Assisting	+	Percent of time it takes client to perform certain kitchen tasks in relation to the time it typically takes other clients.	150%	100%
I	Scheduling	+	Percent of daily scheduled activities that client accomplishes on time without prompting by staff.	100%	75%
I	Setting Goals	–	Number of weekly goals client lists for self.	0	1 (2)
I	Reinforcing	–	Percent of time client rewards or punishes self based on his/her ability to achieve goals set for self.	0%	25% (50%)

Learning Environment: Adult Education Class at halfway house

PEI	Skill Activity	+/-	Skill Behavior	Present	Needed
I	Paying Attention	+	Percent of time client looks directly at instructor when instructor is speaking.	50%	50%
E	Listening	+	Percent of time client can repeat main points of instructor's presentation when called upon.	50%	50%
E	Conversation	–	Number of times client talks (one second or more) with either instructor or classmates during class session.	0	2

Working Environment: Not applicable at present

The final method of collecting information relevant to quantifying the client's needed level of functioning is also the most common method (i.e., asking significant others in these environments what level of functioning is needed). Significant others include treatment personnel, relatives, employers, teachers, and so forth. The practitioner can read the assessment statement to these significant others and ask for their assessment of the client's needed skill level. For example, the estimates of the needed skill level for all skills in Table 25 could be provided by either personnel from the day hospital or the halfway house. When the client's environmental settings include home, school, or work, the relatives', teachers', and employers' estimates of needed level of functioning will also be appropriate.

When two estimates of a needed skill level are conflicting, it makes sense to record both measures; then consider the less-demanding estimate as a short-term goal and the more difficult estimate as a long-term goal. Once the client attains the simpler skill level, it should be clear whether or not she or he still needs to obtain a higher level of functioning. In Table 25, for example, the rehabilitation practitioner and the day-care personnel differ in terms of the client's necessary skill levels of setting goals and reinforcing self. The rehabilitation practitioner estimated a higher level of needed skills than did the day-care personnel. Once the sample client's rehabilitation program has achieved the less-demanding goal, the question of whether or not to work toward the higher level goal can be reevaluated.

If the practitioner wishes to reassess the client in terms of a different environmental setting, she or he can construct a new Client Assessment Chart that identifies the new environments and categorizes and assesses relevant skill behaviors. By the same token, any reduction in environments means a corresponding reduction in relevant skill behaviors. For example, if the adult education class in Table 25 is considered inappropriate at the present time, these behaviors are eliminated from the chart and the number of skill deficits that must be treated are reduced.

When new environments are considered, the process is more complex. For example, if the practitioner and/or the client in Table 25 wish(es) to consider what deficits must be overcome before the client can attend a sheltered workshop rather than the day hospital and adult education class, a new Client Assessment Chart must be constructed. Skill deficit behaviors relevant *only* to the day hospital or adult education class would be eliminated or, if appropriate, redefined to reflect the demands of the new environment. In Table 25, this process would be handled by first identifying which skill behaviors were relevant only to the day hospital and then determining whether or not variations on these behaviors might not also be needed in the workshop setting. As an example, the skills of grooming, traveling, and scheduling from Table 25 have been redefined in Table 26 under working environment. The skills of setting goals and reinforcing self have been eliminated since these were behaviors demanded specifically at the day hospital.

Once the existing skill behaviors on a chart have been either eliminated, redefined, or left on the chart, the practitioner will want to identify the unique demands of the new environment and decide whether or not the client is presently functioning at the level needed to enter the new environment. This new assessment procedure is best handled by interviewing the person who is in charge of this environment, by writing assessment statements based on this person's input, by quantifying the client's needed skill level in these areas, by quantifying the client's present level, and indicating each skill as a strength or deficit depending on whether or not there is a discrepancy between the client's present and needed levels of functioning.

In Table 26, the skills listed under working environment were suggested during a discussion between the practitioner and the workshop director. These are part of a larger list of behaviors that was reduced in number because it was known that the client could already perform some of these behaviors. (For example, workshop employees in this particular workshop should be able to arrive for work each day five to fifteen minutes early; the sample client already has the required skills in this area.) Only those skill areas in which the client's ability is questionable are included on these additional charts. Once the practitioner has written assessment statements and quantified the needed level of functioning, the client's present level is assessed for the skills in question. In the assessment of new environments, the diagnostic emphasis is more on deficits than on strengths; it is the recognition of which deficits must be built into strengths that will play the determining role in the client's move to a more-demanding environment.

The client's ability to function in *any* specific environment can be assessed at this time in the diagnostic planning process. Notice that this reassessment step occurs after the tentative environments for which the client had originally been referred have been assessed. That is, the first assessment process is undertaken for those environments that were suggested either by the referral source or by the client's unique situation. By way of example, suppose the client in Table 26 and/or the referral source had first wanted to consider full-time competitive employment as the working environment. Even though the practitioner may consider this environment too difficult at present based on the client's past behavior, the practitioner could still conduct the initial diagnostic planning process for such an environment and then later (if necessary) reassess the client's functioning for a less-demanding working environment. In this way, the practitioner will have attended to the initial requests of the referral source and the client. Having done this, the practitioner can rationally and observably suggest the reasons why the initial environment is perhaps not as suitable as an alternative setting. Thus, if the client depicted in Table 26 had been originally referred or desired to be assessed with respect to full-time employment, the assessment process would probably have indi-

Table 26.
New Sample Client Assessment Chart Detailing Skills Needed in Working Environment

CLIENT ASSESSMENT CHART   Name _____

Situational Problem: Being discharged from inpatient status.

Rehabilitation Goal: To arrange to live in a halfway house.
To work in a sheltered workshop.

PEI	Skill Activity	+/-	Skill Behavior	Level of Functioning Present	Level of Functioning Needed
Living Environment: Halfway House					
P	Housework	-	Number of room-cleaning behaviors client performs each day from list of 3 appropriate room-cleaning behaviors (make bed, sweep floor, pick up clothes)	2	3
E	Conversation	+	Number of interactions per day lasting 30 seconds or more client performs with people with whom he is living	20	10
E	Control Temper	+	Number of crying-yelling outbursts per week client exhibits during evenings and nights	1	1
E	Speaking Up	-	Number of times per meeting client can speak about self or environment in halfway house or day hospital without being called upon	0	2
I	Kitchen Assisting	-	Percent of time it takes client to perform certain kitchen tasks in relation to the time it typically takes other clients	150%	100%

PEI	+/-	Skill Behavior	Level of Functioning	
Skill Activity			Present	Needed
Learning Environment: Adult Education Class				
P Paying Attention	+	Percent of time client looks directly at instructor when instructor is speaking	50%	50%
E Listening	+	Percent of time client can repeat main points of instructor's presentation when called upon	50%	50%
E Conversation	-	Number of times client talks (one second or more) with either instructor or classmates during class session	0	2
Working Environment: Sheltered Workshop				
P Grooming	+	Number of days per week client can dress and wash self at a level rated as "acceptable" by Workshop Supervisor	5	5
P Traveling	-	Amount of time client takes to travel from halfway house to workshop	unable	25'
P Job Endurance	-	Length of time client can work on one task without break	10'	30'
E Expressing Needs	-	Percent of time client can verbally state what he needs	50%	100%
I Scheduling	+	Percent of workshop activities which client can get to on time	100%	90%
I Following Directions	-	Percent of time client can carry out simple verbal directions	50%	90%

cated that, although the client possessed a certain number of strengths, a great many additional deficits would have to be overcome before the client could function in this environment. Some of the skill deficits that would probably have been diagnosed include job-interviewing skills, job-endurance skills, job-seeking skills, job-maintenance skills, and career-choice skills. These are much more complex and difficult behaviors than those required in a sheltered workshop environment and would involve a much larger rehabilitation treatment program. By assessing this nonsheltered work environment first, the referral source and/or client could see exactly what was needed in order to function in a competitive employment situation. As a matter of fact, programs to overcome many of the above skill deficits could be developed in the sheltered workshop environment. In this way, the competitive employment setting could eventually be attained once the client had developed the ability to function in a sheltered workshop setting.

There are obviously many variations on this same theme. The point is, however, that meaningful comparisons of environmental alternatives involve first assessing the client in terms of the tentative environments that were initially suggested by the referral source and/or the client and then proceeding to assess other possible environmental settings. In this way, the client's ability to meet the skill demands of each environment can be compared and treatment decisions made on the basis of observable data. If the client is placed in a less-demanding environment, the deficits assessed for the more-demanding environment can become areas of treatment intervention.

Based on a comprehensive rehabilitation diagnosis, staff working in an environment may accept a client, knowing full well that the client does not have all the skills necessary to function immediately in the environment. However, if the diagnostic planning process has been carried out thoroughly, this staff will know exactly what skills need to be worked on. Thus, the client *may* be able to move to a new environment (rather than be treated for that deficit in the present environment) as long as the rehabilitation diagnostician informs the receiving environment of deficits that will affect the client's functioning in that environment.

Practice Situation

Now practice quantifying the client's needed level of functioning by using the assessment statements that you redefined in Table 23 and then quantified in terms of present level of functioning on a Client Assessment Chart (Table 24). Indicate on a separate sheet of paper the method you would use to quantify the client's needed level. In other words, do you think the information would be available from the practitioner, the client, or significant others?

Another way you can improve your ability to quantify needed levels of client functioning and simultaneously quantify new possible environments is to use the assessments of your own skill behaviors that you have previously written and quantified. In order to practice this step, perform it with several variations. Quantify your needed skill levels in the learning environment in which you are presently functioning. Imagine that the living environment in which you are eventually going to function is less demanding than your present skill level (i.e., a halfway house or some other sheltered living situation). In contrast, imagine that your next working environment will be more demanding than your present position (i.e., the next job in your career ladder or some job you would possibly like to have). Construct a sample Client Assessment Chart for your present learning environment and for these alternative living and working environments. Then examine the existing skill behaviors already listed in these environments and either eliminate or redefine them or leave them unchanged. Interview the persons who are knowledgeable with respect to these new environments. Write assessment statements based on these persons' input. Quantify the needed levels in these skill areas. Quantify your present levels in these skill areas. Finally, record on the Client Assessment Chart any strength or deficit ratings that occur in each skill area.

Now that you have had the opportunity to practice quantifying with a hypothetical client and with yourself, begin to quantify an actual client's needed level of functioning for initial and alternative environments. Once you have recorded these numbers on the Client Assessment Chart, you have completed the rehabilitation diagnostic assessment process. At this point the client and other interested people are given, by means of the Client Assessment Chart, a graphic analysis of exactly what needs to be achieved in order to maximize the possibility of rehabilitation success.

Not only throughout the diagnostic process but especially at this point (because of the impact of the Client Assessment Chart), the rehabilitation practitioner may wish to check out the client's and significant others' responses to the assessment in order to make sure that it is understandable. The danger in presenting diagnoses of any type to people is that they hear only the first part of what is being said; the reality of the diagnosis often triggers thoughts that keep them from listening to all aspects of the assessment. Thus, the interviewer's skills of responding are needed again at the end of the diagnostic planning process; the diagnostic planning process begins, continues, and ends with the responding skills of the rehabilitation practitioner.

QUANTIFYING THE CLIENT'S NEEDED LEVEL OF FUNCTIONING: A SUMMARY

Goal: To estimate as exactly as possible the client's needed level of functioning in diagnosed skill areas.

1. Operationalize the client's previously diagnosed skills.

2. Estimate the client's present level of functioning.

3. Estimate the client's needed level of functioning by using information previously collected during the diagnostic planning process;

   and/or

4. Obtain the client's estimate of his or her needed level of functioning;

   and/or

5. Ask significant others to estimate the client's needed level of functioning.

6. If conflicting estimates occur, use the lower estimate as a short-term goal.

7. If the client is to be reassessed for a different environment skill, behaviors relevant to that environment must first be diagnosed and then tasks 1-6 repeated for these newly diagnosed skills.

ASSESSING: A SKILLED APPROACH

Sheila looked over Bob's shoulder at the list of specific deficits and assets that they had spent the last several sessions developing.

"We're agreed, then," she said. "One major goal has got to be to get control of your temper. That's a problem that you have found in every area — living with your family, going to night school, working, everywhere."

Bob nodded. "Yeah, there's not much question about that." His eyes met Sheila's as she came around to sit facing him again. "I've told you how it is. I'm okay for a while. But then things start happening. Little things — like maybe my car won't start in the morning, or my sister used up the last of the cereal, or my boss says something to me that gets under my skin. And wham! I feel this pressure building up in me until — well, I guess I just fly off the handle!" He shook his head and looked away unhappily.

"You feel pretty helpless when you can't control your own temper," Sheila agreed. "I think the first thing we've got to do is decide exactly what 'keeping your temper' really means."

"What it means? Doesn't it just mean — well, not getting mad anymore?" Sheila nodded. "Sure. Except that phrases like 'losing your tem-

per' and 'getting mad' don't really tell you enough. What kinds of things do you **do** when you lose your temper?"

"Oh…" Bob thought about this. "Well, I guess what I almost always do is end up hitting someone or something…" He looked away sheepishly. "Like that last big blowup where I ended up hitting my foreman at work."

Sheila nodded. "Right. That's what I thought. Well, then, we might say that your goal is to keep your temper. And you'll know you've reached this goal when you can keep from physically hitting anyone or anything — not even kicking your car if it doesn't want to start!"

This made sense to Bob. "At least that'll let me know exactly when I'm making it and when I'm messing up, huh?"

"Sure," Sheila agreed. "You feel a lot more confident when you've got a really clear target to aim at!"

Sheila knew that although developing and defining a goal in clear, sharp, and tangible terms was the last stage of the diagnostic planning process, it was only the first stage of a longer process. She would have to help Bob develop an adequate number of equally clear and tangible steps leading to the goal. She would have to make sure each step was supported by appropriate reinforcements that would help Bob stay on track. She would have to outline specific ways of evaluating his progress.

The goal was just the first stage. But without a clear-cut goal, Sheila knew that none of the subsequent stages could even begin. And Sheila was a firm believer in the idea that things usually end well only if they begin well!

Chapter 5 DIAGNOSTIC PLANNING WITH SIGNIFICANT OTHERS ▮

DIAGNOSTIC PLANNING WITH SIGNIFICANT OTHERS: AN UNSKILLED APPROACH

"Hello?..."

"Hello, Mrs. James?" Betty put down her pen in order to concentrate her attention more fully on the call. "This is Betty Smith at the Hopkins Clinic. I've been working with Mark..."

"Oh, yes — Mark has talked about you quite often..." To Betty's ears the other woman's voice sounded uncertain, hesitant. "Is there some — some problem about Mark?"

"No, Mrs. James — as far as I can tell from Mark's conversations with me, everything's been fine since he went home from the hospital. I actually called to see if you might be able to come in and talk with me about Mark. I've usually found that this is a good way to make sure no problems do come up. If you have half an hour or so later this week, I think we could help each other and Mark at the same time by having a talk."

"Oh — well, yes, that sounds fine." Mrs. James was clearly relieved to hear that Mark wasn't in any new trouble — and happy to be offered a chance to share her 'side' of the situation involving her son. Betty had no trouble arranging a date with her for that Thursday afternoon. She made sure to give the older woman clear directions on how to reach her office. Hanging up at last, she had a pleasant feeling of accomplishment.

"That's that," she said to herself with satisfaction. But unfortunately it wasn't.

Mrs. James arrived on schedule Thursday afternoon — a small, nervous woman who obviously cared a great deal about her son yet at the same time worried about her own ability to make things work out now that he was home. According to her, things were going well but far from perfectly. After some hedging, she got to the point.

*"He doesn't **do** anything," Mrs. James complained. "I mean, I know he's been — sick. But sometimes it just seems like he's using that as an excuse to get out of — oh, just everything. He doesn't make his bed, he doesn't cook for himself like he used to, he hardly even goes out of the house. All he does is sit around watching TV or reading silly magazines!"*

Betty hadn't bothered to plan her conference with Mrs. James in any great detail. Her only thought had been to see Mark's mother and have a good general talk with her. Yet here was a fairly clear problem —

and one that Mark himself had not seen fit to mention. Well, Betty would have to take it up with him, no question about it.

Yet it turned out to be difficult if not impossible to get a constructive response from Mark the next time he came in for his regular session.

"My mother told you I wasn't doing enough?" His voice was shrill with protest. "I can't believe it!" Then he seemed to calm down a bit. "But then again, I guess I can believe it. You don't know her the way I do. Mom's great, don't get me wrong. But she tends to be — well, kind of neurotic about some things. Like neatness, for example. She's one of those people who cover sofas with plastic so they won't get messed up — empties every ashtray as soon as someone flicks one ash in it — like that." Mark laughed ruefully. "Poor Mom — I bet she had the time of her life laying all that sob story on you!"

All of this left Betty in a difficult position, to say the least. Was Mark telling the truth? Was his mother really just a neurotically compulsive person unloading on her son? Or had Mrs. James been telling the truth? Was Mark actually taking advantage of his mother's sympathy to live a cushy life?

Then another thought occurred to Betty. Regardless of who was telling the truth, how was Mark going to react to his mother now that he knew she had accused him of "not doing things"? Betty found herself hoping fervently that this latest development would not upset the precarious balance Mark had achieved at home.

What had gone wrong? All Betty had wanted to do was have a little chat with Mark's mother. How could such a simple, general aim have such potentially disastrous consequences?

For the life of her, Betty couldn't think of an answer to this question.

Up to this point, this text has focused on working only with the client. That is, we have addressed the diagnostic interviewing skills needed by the practitioner to facilitate *exploration* and *understanding* on the client's part and, in this way, to arrive at a comprehensive and comprehensible *assessment* of the client. Clearly, however, no client lives in a vacuum. Other people such as family, friends, employers, or other treatment personnel may significantly affect the life of the client. Because the goal of rehabilitation is to promote or at least maintain the client's ability to function in specific environments, the practitioner has to be knowledgeable about these environments. Thus, in almost all cases, the rehabilitation practitioner will find it necessary to interact with significant others in the client's environment.

The timing and type of involvement that the practitioner has with significant other people varies considerably depending upon what the practitioner's goals are in contacting these people. There are essentially three reasons for interacting with significant others, which reasons parallel the diagnostic planning process with the client: *exploration, understanding,* and/or *assessment.*

Many of the experiences the client explores will involve one or more of these significant other people. In order to understand more fully what is expected from the client in his or her world and to make a more accurate diagnosis of the client's role in the problem, the practitioner will want to obtain information about the client's strengths and deficits from the significant others who are so much a part of the client's world. Research evidence exists that shows that the client's family can provide important information about the client that does not duplicate information explored by the client (Schless & Mendels, 1978; Walls & Masson, 1978).

The practitioner will want to facilitate the *exploration* by these people of experiences that they may have had with the client. In some cases, as with the spouse of an alcoholic client, it may well be appropriate to help the significant other person *understand* his or her role in the problems jointly experienced by him or her and the client.

In many cases, the practitioner will want to use the input of significant others to help her or him and the client *assess* the client's present and needed levels of functioning. To reach these goals of exploration, understanding, and/or assessment with significant others, the practitioner can apply some or all of the same diagnostic planning skills used with the client: attending, responding, personalizing, categorizing, and assessing. The remainder of this chapter will focus on the application of these skills to interactions with significant others. For the sake of clarity, these environmental diagnostic skills have been discussed in this separate chapter; the involvement of significant others, however, may occur at any point throughout the diagnostic planning process — depending, of course, on the purpose of involving the significant others.

EXPLORING WITH SIGNIFICANT OTHERS

The main purpose of engaging significant others in exploration is to obtain further information about the client's strengths and deficits. A secondary purpose is to ascertain if the significant other person may have possible strengths and deficits in relation to the client. If this seems likely, the practitioner will have to attempt to personalize, categorize, and assess these particular strengths and deficits so that they may be addressed in the rehabilitation treatment program.

To facilitate exploration with significant others, the practitioner should use the same skills that he or she used to facilitate the client's exploration: informing, encouraging, attending, observing, listening, responding, and specifying. The goal here is to facilitate the significant other's exploration at levels 2 and 3 on the five-point Diagnostic Interviewing Process Scale (see Chapter 3). At level 2, the significant other person will be able to explore the who, what, where, when, why, and how of the particular situation. At this level of exploration, the significant other will be focusing on the client and not on the personal meaning of the situation for him or herself. At level 3, the significant other will be discussing the client's situation in terms of how it makes the significant other feel. At these levels of exploration, the significant other will be disclosing valuable information that either corroborates or adds to the information already gathered from the client.

Because the practitioner's skills that facilitate exploration by significant others are the same skills that facilitate client self-exploration, the discussion of these skills will not be repeated in great detail. However, several specific points do need to be mentioned. The first of these points involves how to go about contacting significant others. As a general rule, all contacts with significant others should first be cleared with the client. The client should be told the purpose of the contacts; and the practitioner should respond to the client's reaction to the possible contact. The client may have good reasons for the practitioner not contacting significant others and his or her wishes must be respected.

Assuming that contact is appropriate, the practitioner must then decide whether the contact need be face-to-face or whether a telephone call will do. If the practitioner wishes to explore the client's situation fully with the significant other, a face-to-face meeting is usually desirable. This personal contact itself communicates that the issue is important and encourages the significant other person to express him or herself. In addition, the personal attention that can be communicated through physically attending also facilitates the verbal expression of the significant other.

If personal contact is desirable, the practitioner must decide whether to go to the significant other or whether the other person should be invited to come to the practitioner. This decision will depend upon the amount of time the significant other has invested in the client. The client may have had prior contact with a therapist, for example, yet may represent only a small part of this therapist's treatment responsibility. In such a case, it may be appropriate for the practitioner to speak to the therapist over the telephone. If the significant other is a member of the client's immediate family with a large investment in the client, however, it is probably appropriate to ask the person to come to the practitioner.

Whether the appointment is to be held at the office of the practitioner or at a place more convenient to the significant other person, the invitation (request) will establish the *purpose* of the meeting (why) and the *time* and *place* (when and where). Beyond these basics, anything that is added in terms of encouragement or directions (how) will be based on the individual needs of the other person. In general, significant others who are family members or friends will often have to be treated like the client (e.g., encouragement and directions should be added). Significant others who have a more professional relationship (therapist, workshop supervisor, potential employer) will need different types of encouragement.

Suppose, for example, the practitioner wishes to see the wife of a client who is preparing to be discharged from the hospital and return home. The practitioner knows that the client's wife has visited him on a number of occasions in the hospital; she clearly knows where it is. The practitioner's invitation for the initial exploratory visit might be as follows:

"I would like to meet with you at three in the afternoon, next Thursday, here in my office, to discuss your husband's current situation. It is important that we meet because we have found that when the patient's family is involved with us, the patient's return home is much smoother.

"I look forward to meeting with you. If you check with the receptionist in Room 409, she will direct you to my office."

Here the practitioner gives the client's wife information concerning what will be done, when, and where. The practitioner goes on to encourage the client's wife to appear by indicating a potential benefit of her appearance.

Practice Situations

Think about a client with whom you are currently working. Then think about a significant other (perhaps a family member, friend, employer, or treatment professional) whom it would be appropriate for you to see regarding this client. Write down what you might say to this person to schedule him or her for an appointment. Check your response to be sure it includes at least the purpose of the meeting as well as when and where. Then check to make sure you have given the person any other information that she or he may require — including encouragement to appear.

INTERVIEWING THE SIGNIFICANT OTHER

Once the significant other person appears, the practitioner works to involve that person in expressing him or herself. The skills employed here are the same contextual and personal attending skills described in Chapter 2. Briefly, the practitioner must first prepare his or her office to receive the person, then attend to the physical needs of the person, and finally communicate interest and attention by employing attending, observing, and listening skills. These steps are followed whether the significant other is a treatment professional, an employer, or a member of the client's family.

Once these attending steps have been completed and the significant other has become involved in the interaction, the practitioner is ready to enter the responding phase of the interview. It will be recalled that the overall goal of responding is to facilitate self-exploration by another person. More specifically, there are two areas for exploration:

the particular situation in which the person is involved and his or her feelings about the situation. As a general rule, responding to content facilitates exploration of the situation itself. Responding to feelings increases exploration of the effect related to the situation. And responding to feeling and content facilitates exploration of both the experience and the related feelings. Finally, questions can be used to fill in gaps concerning the who, what, when, where, why, and how of the situation.

The particular mode of responding used with significant others will depend upon the exploration desired. If all the practitioner wants is a description of the situation (level 2, self-exploration), he or she will primarily use responses to content. If exploration of the feelings and the situation are appropriate (level 3, self-exploration), the practitioner will want to respond to both elements of the experience. In general, responses to treatment personnel and employers will emphasize content while responses to family and friends will more often address both feeling and content. The reason is that the latter groups are more likely to be intimately involved with the client and, therefore, are more likely to have feelings in these areas where their lives intersect with the client's. This is only a general guideline, of course. At times it will definitely be appropriate to respond to the feelings of treatment professionals or employers concerning their experience with the client. By the same token, a family member who is wary of discussing feelings might better be approached initially by responses to content.

As an example, read the following interaction between a rehabilitation practitioner and a halfway house director concerning a client with whom they were both involved. The purpose of the contact is to explore how well the client has been able to function in a new rehabilitation environment:

Director: *"Harold's been pretty withdrawn since he's been with us. He takes care of himself and his belongings, but very seldom volunteers anything—even in group. About the only time he talks is when someone asks him a direct question."*

Practitioner: *"You're saying, then, that although Harold does what is expected of him, he's still pretty much in his shell."*

Director: *"Yeah, for a while I thought he was going to come out of it, but then this guy whom he seemed to be closest to left. I've really tried a number of times to get next to Harold, but he's just so distant. It's tough!"*

Practitioner: *"With the way Harold seems, I guess it's pretty frustrating to try to build a relationship with him."*

In the first statement, the practitioner responds only to the content of the director's statement. But as it becomes evident that the director

148

has personal feelings about his experience with the client, the practitioner also responds to these.

Practice Situations

Now use your skills to respond to the statements below.

Background: *You have asked the married daughter of a fifty-five-year-old male outpatient to come to see you for purposes of exploration. Her father lives with her and her husband. She has been talking about ten or fifteen minutes when the statement below is made:*

Statement 1: *"Dad is so tired. He used to be so full of energy, but now he doesn't get up 'til afternoon. Even when he's up, he doesn't want to do anything. It's so different from the way he used to be before he was hospitalized."*

Respond to the daughter's first statement.

Statement 2: *"For a while, I thought he'd get back to work. But now I wonder if he ever will. It's been almost four months now."*

Respond to the daughter's second statement.

It would probably be appropriate to respond to both the feeling and the content for each of these expressions. The response to the first statement can be along the lines of, "You feel sad because your Dad just isn't the person he used to be." The response to the second statement can be similar to, "You feel worried because it's not clear when it will end."

As a follow-up to this exercise, you can practice responding to those significant other people with whom you interact on behalf of your clients. As you respond, be sure to note the effect on their willingness to explore the situation with you and to disclose client strengths and deficits to you.

UNDERSTANDING THE SIGNIFICANT OTHER'S STRENGTHS AND DEFICITS

Although intent on facilitating the significant other's exploration, the practitioner must also decide whether the significant other can personalize his or her role in helping the client achieve the rehabilitation goals. That is, besides verifying and/or extending the list of the client's strengths and deficits, the practitioner might try to identify any behaviors of significant others that could play an important role in helping or hindering the client's ability to function in a particular environment. Typically, those significant others are the client's immediate family and friends. In some instances, however, it may be another professional who needs to alter her or his behaviors in order to facilitate the client's attainment of rehabilitation goals.

In deciding whether or not to personalize the significant other's understanding, the practitioner must be guided by several factors. With some significant others, the practitioner may have decided to attempt to personalize even before meeting the significant others. This could be a function of previous information about the significant other that suggests to the practitioner that the significant other is not being as facilitative as possible. In such cases, the practitioner must be sure to be as responsive as possible before initiating a personalized interpretation.

In other situations, the decision of whether or not to personalize may be "made" for the practitioner by the significant other. Various statements that some significant others make are clear invitations to personalize. These include such statements as, *"I just don't know what to do;"* or, *"I wish I could be more helpful."* Other people will begin to move themselves toward personalized understanding: (1) *"I don't want to lose her. She's too good a worker."* (2) *"If he doesn't shape up, I'm going to kick him out — but the thought of doing that just kills me."* (3) *"I just can't seem to get her to change. She refuses to see it my way."* In all three of these examples, the significant other is beginning to self-explore at level 4.0 or 5.0 on the five-point Diagnostic Interviewing Process Scale.

In the following example of exploring and understanding, the practitioner interviews the mother of a fourteen-year-old emotionally disturbed boy. This is the mother's second interview with the practitioner.

Mother: *"My other two kids are just fine, but Freddie just runs everybody ragged. He's never still — always into everything. He's just impossible to manage."*

Practitioner: *"You really feel burdened by the constant strain of trying to handle this kid."* (Interchangeable response to feeling and content)

Mother: *"I know it sounds like a terrible thing to say, but it's been like having a monkey in the house. He's all over and things are always being broken and torn down."*

Practitioner: *"Even though you're saying you feel guilty about saying it, you really have experienced him as behaving like an animal."* (Interchangeable response to feeling and content)

Mother: *"It's just like all his life I've had to be on guard. There's never a moment's rest. Even the medicine never slowed him down much."*

Practitioner:	*"You feel overwhelmed because you have your whole life — every minute — revolving around your son."* (Response to feeling and personalized meaning)
Mother:	*"It's like I'm just being dragged down by Freddie. I don't know what to do anymore."*
Practitioner:	*"You're getting scared because you can't identify any realistic alternatives for getting some relief from Freddie."* (Response to feelings and personalized deficit)
Mother:	*"I know I can't take it anymore — not all the time, anyway — but I don't know what else to do with him."*

After responding to the mother, the practitioner interprets the meaning of the situation for the mother and then goes on to pinpoint at least one deficit that is contributing to the problem — her inability to identify an alternative to her problem in caring for the child. At the same time, the practitioner diagnoses the mother's level of desperation caused by her behavioral deficit. This information will be critical in designing an overall rehabilitation plan for the family.

Practice Situations

Now work with the young man presented below. Use the first three expressions to lay a responsive base for personalizing; then interpret the personalized meaning after the fourth statement, and finally interpret the personalized problem after the fifth statement.

Background:	*Sam is a young man whose wife went into a severe suicidal depression after having their third child in less than five years. She has been depressed for almost four months while he struggles to work and care for the family.*
Sam's Statement 1:	*"It doesn't ever seem to change. She gets up for a few days or even a week or two, then she goes back down again. It's like being on a roller-coaster."*
Sam's Statement 2:	*"She's up and around when I leave for work and seems to be doing okay ... but I come home and nothing has been done. The house is a mess. The kids are crying. I don't even always know if she is feeding them."*

151

<table>
<tr><td align="right">*Sam's*
Statement 3:</td><td>*"Maybe it's wrong of me — I don't know — but I really get sick of her not carrying her end of the load."*</td></tr>
<tr><td align="right">*Sam's*
Statement 4:</td><td>*"I never had a real family when I was a kid and when I got married I was really looking forward to having a family of my own. But it's sure gone sour."*</td></tr>
<tr><td align="right">*Sam's*
Statement 5:</td><td>*"I try to show her I care about her and everything. But then when she doesn't improve, I get mad and start yelling. Deep down I know she needs my support, but I just can't help myself."*</td></tr>
</table>

In the case above, it is clear that Sam must deal with his own reaction to his wife's problem if they, as individuals and as a couple, are going to be restored to a healthy state.

CATEGORIZING ENVIRONMENTAL STRENGTHS AND DEFICITS

If the practitioner has identified the strengths and deficits of various significant others, the next phase of the understanding process is to categorize the strengths and deficits with respect to whether these behaviors will primarily affect the client's living, learning, and/or working environment.

Table 27 presents a list of possible environmental strengths and deficits that might be critical to a client's rehabilitation outcome. Although such an extensive list would probably not occur for each client, the list does provide some common examples. Indeed, if a client were to try to function in an environment in which these were all deficits, the practitioner would no doubt have some questions about the appropriateness of the environment for the client and/or the amount of time and effort that would have to be invested in improving the client's environment.

In Table 28, these sample environmental strengths and deficits have been categorized as to whether they affect the client's living, learning, and/or working environments. Some of the environmental strengths and deficits were obtained by making personalized interpretations with significant others (e.g., "spouse rarely praises client"). Other environmental strengths and deficits were simply observable facts (e.g., "transportation to school is lacking"). By classifying en-

152

Table 27. Sample of Potential Environmental Strengths and Deficits

Spouse (rarely) praises client.

Parents of client (refuse to) visit client often.

School advisement procedure is good (poor).

Supervisor's directions to client are clear (confusing).

Local school's fees for part-time students are reasonable (excessive).

Employer is willing (reluctant) to rehire client.

Neighbors are comfortable (afraid of) and friendly with (ignore) client.

Treatment professionals are willing (unwilling) to discharge client to partial hospitalization.

Spouse is willing (unwilling) to become involved in the treatment plan.

Child of client is agreeable to (hesitant about) allowing client to live with her.

School provides necessary (no) assistance in securing tutor.

Former co-workers are able (unsure of how) to respond to client.

Transportation to school is available (lacking).

Former employer's letter of recommendation is excellent (poor).

vironmental characteristics in this manner, the practitioner and the client will begin to understand in which environmental areas the client will find support or a lack of support. This data will obviously be used later in formulating a complete diagnostic plan. Even at this early phase in the diagnostic planning process, however, some tentative ideas will begin to emerge about environmental treatment intervention strategies and timing.

Practice Situations

Table 29 is a sample Environmental Diagnostic Planning Chart. This chart, in combination with a chart similar to the Client Diagnostic Planning Chart depicted in Table 23, provides the practitioner and the client with a diagnostic overview of both the *client* and the client's *environment*. Try to think of other common environmental deficits and place them in the appropriate environmental areas of a chart similar to Table 29. Your examples, along with the examples previously mentioned in Table 28, provide you with a good listing of typical environmental deficits.

Table 28.

Sample Environmental Strengths and Deficits Categorized L,L, and W

ENVIRONMENTAL DIAGNOSTIC PLANNING CHART   Name _____

Environment	+	−	Skill Behavior
Living			Spouse (rarely) praises client.
			Parents of client (refuse to) visit client often.
			Neighbors comfortable (afraid of) and friendly with (ignore) client.
			Treatment professionals willing (unwilling) to discharge client to partial hospitalization.
			Spouse willing (unwilling) to become involved in treatment plan.
			Child of client agreeable to (hesitant about) allowing client to live with her.
Learning			School advisement procedure is good (poor).
			Local school fees for part-time students are reasonable (excessive).
			School provides necessary (no) assistance in securing tutor.
			Transportation to school is available (lacking).
Working			Supervisor's directions to client are clear (confusing).
			Employer willing (reluctant) to rehire client.
			Former co-workers able (unsure of how) to respond to client.
			Former employer's letter of recommendation is excellent (poor).

154

Table 29.
Sample Environmental Diagnostic Planning Chart

ENVIRONMENTAL DIAGNOSTIC PLANNING CHART   Name ————————

Situational Problem: ————————

Rehabilitation Goal: ————————

Environment	+ −	Skill Behavior
Living ——— ——— ——— ———		
Learning ——— ——— ———		
Working ——— ——— ———		

155

Now try to categorize the environmental deficits of a client with whom you are presently working. Once again, try to make the process and the language as straightforward and familiar as possible. After these behaviors are categorized, they are like the client's skills, that is, they also need to be assessed.

ASSESSING THE SIGNIFICANT OTHER'S STRENGTHS AND DEFICITS

The practitioner interacts with significant others in the environment for two assessment purposes: to help him or herself assess the client; and to assess the strengths and deficits of the significant others in the client's environment. The assessment of the significant other's strengths and deficits flows directly from the previous understanding of significant others' strengths and deficits. The assessment process and outcome are the same as during client assessment, only this time the practitioner works primarily with the significant other.

Table 30 provides an example of an Environmental Assessment Chart filled out for those characteristics used as examples in Table 28. Note that some of the environmental characteristics could have been obtained simply by telephoning the school or the former employer. Others (such as data about the spouse) could have come from an interview with the spouse. Still others (such as measurements of neighbors and co-workers) could have come from information provided by the client and/or the spouse. Note also that the chart is different from the Client Assessment Chart (Table 23) in that the "who" performing the behavior is specifically indicated. *A completed Environmental Assessment Chart*
(Table 31) and the Client Assessment Chart (Table 23) are the tangible products of the diagnostic planning process.

As indicated above, the other purpose of contacting significant others is to gather assessment information about the client. Information about the client's present or needed level of functioning can often be obtained quickly by contacting significant others and reading to them the relevant items from the Client Assessment Chart. Also, it is often significant others who suggest additional behaviors to be included on the Client Assessment Chart. After the significant other has suggested this behavior, the practitioner and the significant other can proceed to operationalize and quantify the behavior. These assessment steps are necessary because significant others usually talk about the client's present or needed behaviors in general terms. For example, a halfway house director may indicate that this setting tolerates no "acting out" behavior from their clients. The rehabilitation practitioner must then help the director to operationalize what she or he objectively and observably means by this statement. This assessment is then entered on the client's assessment chart under "Skill Activity" and the required level of functioning is inserted under "Needed" level. If this environmental setting becomes a realistic possibility, this skill is subsequently discussed with the client and his or her present level of functioning in this skill is assessed and recorded on the Client Assessment Chart; whether the skill is a strength or deficit is also noted on the chart.

It must be remembered that the practitioner's interactions with significant others are always presented to the client. If environmental deficits are identified and assessed, these are discussed with the client. If significant others suggest new client strengths and deficits and/or make new or different assessments, these are also discussed with the client. The ability of the client to comprehend the diagnostic planning process will obviously vary depending on the severity of the client's symptoms. The goal, however, is always to maximize client understanding in hopes of maximizing client motivation. Thus, at a minimum, the Client Assessment Chart and the Environmental Assessment Chart are always available for the client's examination. The goal of the diagnostic planning process is not simply to diagnose the client but, to the extent possible, to diagnose *with* the client. Thus, the practitioner who, by means of her or his responding, personalizing, categorizing, and assessing skills, has been able to effectively use the input of significant others in the diagnostic planning process will constantly want to strive to make the client aware of this input. In so doing, the practitioner will often stimulate the client to greater depths of exploration and understanding.

Practice Situations

Practice assessing environmental deficits, using as stimuli the additional environmental deficits you added to Table 29. You can use a format similar to Table 31 to record these additions. Next, try to assess the environmental deficits of a client with whom you are currently working. Share these assessments with your client and respond to any exploration that this list helped stimulate.

Table 30.
Sample Environmental Assessment Chart

ENVIRONMENTAL ASSESSMENT CHART   Name _____

Situational Problem: _____

Rehabilitation Goal: _____

Environment	±	Person	Skill Behavior	Level of Functioning	
				Present	Needed
Living					
Home	–	Spouse	Number of times per week spouse praises client when she does something that pleases him	1	15
	+	Parents	Percent of time parents visit client when asked	100%	100%
	–	Neighbors	Number of times next-door neighbors telephone client when client is home on weekend pass	0	2
	+	Therapist	Number of days notice therapist gives before discharging client to partial hospitalization	14	14
	+	Spouse	Number of times per week spouse is willing to meet with rehabilitation practitioner	1	1
	+	Child	Percent of nights client can stay with 30-year-old off-spring when husband is out of town	100%	100%

Environment	±	Person	Skill Behavior	Level of Functioning	
				Present	Needed
Learning					
Community College	+	Advisor	Percent of time advisor will meet with client when requested by client	100%	100%
	–	Registrar	Amount of money charged to take part-time courses	$25 a a credit	$5 a a credit
	+	School Counselor	Number of tutors for special students recruited by counselors who are available in 1 month	20	1
	+	Bus Dispatcher	Amount of time bus ride takes from home to school	15 minutes	less than 1 hour
Working					
Hospital Workshop	+	Workshop Foreman	Percent of time client can follow supervisor's directions	100%	100%
Former Job	+	Former Employer	Length of time former employer is willing to hold job open for client	1 year	6 months
	–	Co-workers	Number of visits per weekend to client from co-worker since the client's hospitalization	0	1
	+	Former Employer	Number of positive letters of recommendation former employer willing to send out	as many as needed	as many as needed

Table 31.
Sample Environmental Assessment Chart

ENVIRONMENTAL ASSESSMENT CHART   Name _____

Situational Problem: _____

Rehabilitation Goal: _____

Environment	±	Person	Skill Behavior	Level of Functioning	
				Present	Needed
Living ___ ___ ___ ___					
Learning ___ ___ ___ ___					
Working ___ ___ ___ ___					

DIAGNOSTIC PLANNING WITH SIGNIFICANT OTHERS: A SUMMARY

Goal: To obtain diagnostic information about the client's strengths and deficits and/or the strengths and deficits of the client's environment.

1. Promote significant others' identification of additional client strengths and deficits by informing, encouraging, attending, observing, listening, and responding to their comments.

2. Obtain any needed client assessment information from significant others.

3. If appropriate, personalize the strengths and deficits of the significant others.

4. Observe for any other environmental strengths and deficits relevant to the client's goals.

5. Categorize on an Environmental Assessment Chart those identified environmental strengths and deficits as to whether they impact the client's living, learning, or working environments.

6. Operationalize and quantify these environmental strengths and deficits.

7. Share diagnostic information collected from significant others with the client.

DIAGNOSTIC PLANNING WITH SIGNIFICANT OTHERS: A SKILLED APPROACH

At first, Mr. Alvarez had been hesitant about coming in to talk with Martha about his wife's situation. Familiar with such hesitancy, however, Martha had explained how such a visit would help make things smoother at home not only for Tessa Alvarez but for her husband as well. This had done the trick; Mr. Alvarez had listened carefully to Martha's directions on how to reach her office. And he had appeared a full five minutes early for their meeting.

Martha was ready for him. She had prepared for their conference by outlining on paper Tessa Alvarez's assets, deficits, and present and needed levels of functioning.

"You know your wife has been getting outpatient care because of her really strong feelings of depression during the last year or so." Mr. Alvarez nodded his understanding. "What I'd like to do is go over the particular things Tessa and I have decided are important right now — both her strong points and her weak ones. We've explored a number of areas where she has real problems and we've laid out definite steps she can take to overcome each of these problems. I'd like to talk about each of these problems with you and hear how you feel Tessa is doing in working to overcome them."

"Sure, of course," Mr. Alvarez nodded. "Listen, I want to do anything I can to help Tes!"

Martha then proceeded to lay out each problem area and the operationalized goals that accompanied each problem. Mr. Alvarez listened carefully and told Martha what Tessa's progress looked like from his point of view. As it turned out, the picture of Tessa that Martha had developed was an accurate one.

"It's really good — she's gone back to cooking really good meals, just like she used to. And I help her out with them, too, just like I used to," he said at one point. And later: "Yeah, she shows a lot of care for me and her children — not like last summer when she just laid around and looked unhappy so much of the time!"

Things looked good. Yet as Mr. Alvarez continued to explore his wife's activities from his own vantage point, he stumbled across one thing that seemed to bother him.

"She still doesn't talk to anyone outside the house," he told Martha. "At home she seems real happy. But she won't even go next door to Mrs. Svoboda's like she used to. It's — I don't know — it's like she's scared to open up to anyone except the family."

Hearing the concern in Mr. Alvarez's voice, Martha helped him to explore this area more fully. Reduced to its simplest and most operational terms, Tessa's difficulty was eventually stated by her husband as, "She can't even say 'hello' to anyone outside the house."

Next, Martha helped Mr. Alvarez to personalize the situation in terms that put him back into the picture. Beginning with responses like, "You feel worried because Tessa can't even greet anyone outside the family," Martha was eventually able to help him accept some of the responsibility: "You feel confused because you can't seem to give Tessa the confidence she needs to greet others."

The problem was Tessa's. But now it was also her husband's. With Martha's help, he began to see that Tessa's lack of confidence might be due in significant part to his own failure to praise her for her increasingly constructive and positive efforts within the home.

"I never thought about that," he said. "I don't know, I guess I just got into the habit of taking the good for granted and only worrying about the bad. I can see now that that kind of thing probably wasn't doing Tessa any good.

Martha nodded. "It's surprising how often the simplest things, the things right under our noses, are exactly what we overlook." She went on to help Mr. Alvarez to set a goal of his own — to build up his wife's confidence by praising her at least once a day for the things she did do well. Together they developed a set of specific steps to reach this goal. When Mr. Alvarez finally left, Martha relaxed in her chair with a sigh of satisfaction.

It wasn't that everything was done. There would be additional contacts with Mr. Alvarez — and later, perhaps, with some potential employers if Tessa continued to progress. Yet everything was under con-

trol and moving forward. Martha would see Tessa the next day and talk of her meeting with Tessa's husband. She felt sure that Tessa would be able to work out this newly revealed problem. And she felt sure that her own abilities would continue to make it possible for her to help Tessa.

Chapter 6 EVALUATING THE EFFECTIVENESS OF THE DIAGNOSTIC PLANNING PROCESS

The effectiveness of diagnostic planning is potentially measurable in terms of both *process* and *outcome*. At an outcome level, the ultimate measure of diagnostic success is the degree to which a diagnostic plan is developed that is actually used for treatment leading to real-life benefits for the client. More specifically, the diagnostic plan (1) contains goals that the client and significant others actually try to achieve; and (b) ensures that these goals are such that attainment of them results in observable and measurable benefits in the lives of both the client and significant others. Thus, one outcome measure of the effectiveness of the diagnostic plan would be the number and/or percentage of set goals that are achieved by the client and significant others. A second outcome measure would be whether or not the attainment of these goals makes a real difference in the things that were the larger client problems (e.g., time in the hospital, ability to hold a job, satisfaction with spouse and/or children).

Clearly, then, the real effectiveness of the diagnostic plan cannot be known until the completion of the rehabilitation process. However, the effectiveness of the diagnostic planning can be evaluated at a process level in two different ways: (1) by examining the diagnostic interview process; and (2) by examining the diagnostic plan (i.e., the Client Assessment Chart and the Environmental Assessment Chart).

At the interview level, there are two basic ways by which the effectiveness of the diagnostic interview can be assessed. One method involves looking at the client's behavior. The second method examines the skill of the practitioner. Both of these sources of analysis can be evaluated through the use of five-point scales.

The client scale looks at the level at which the client explores and understands his or her experience. The scale is the same Diagnostic Interviewing Scale (Table 12) that was described and discussed in Chapter 3. The scale is presented on the following page.

In using the client scale, it is possible to rate at the midpoint of each level (i.e., 1.5, 2.5, 3.5, and 4.5). For example, if the client is not exploring with emotional proximity, or only in vague abstract terms, it is appropriate to deduct half a level.

When you use the rating scale, you will want to look at the interview as a whole and rate how far the client got in relation to each topic. For example, did the client just reach the point where she or he would talk about the situation or did she or he explore the skill deficits that were interfering with reaching personal goals?

Client Diagnostic Interviewing Scale

Level 1.0   The client *does not discuss any relevant material.* He or she either does not express him or herself at all or talks only about situations that have no relevance to the rehabilitation situation.

Level 2.0   The client *discusses material about relevant situations.* He or she explores the who, what, where, when, why, and how of the particular situation.

Level 3.0   The client *discusses material about relevant situations and his or her feelings* concerning these situations. He or she explores this material with emotional proximity (i.e., says things the way she or he feels them).

Level 4.0   The client *discusses material concerning the personal meaning* of the situations with which he or she is faced. That is, the client talks about why the experiences she or he is having are personally important. Again, he or she explores this material with emotional proximity.

Level 5.0   The client *discusses material concerning the personalized strengths and deficits* she or he has. That is, the client works to identify the specific personal strengths or deficits relevant to her or his rehabilitation situation. The client's attempts to understand this material are marked by emotional proximity.

Below are five excerpts that have been rated. Look at them as examples of scale ratings.

Excerpt 1:   *"Well, my car has been acting up the last couple of weeks. First the window was stuck, then the blinker light didn't work, then the muffler started rusting out. Cars are something else."*

Rating: *1.0*

Excerpt 2:   *"I've been really trying to get a job. The employment service has sent me out on three interviews but so far nothing. They ask what I've been doing since I've been out of work and when I say I've been in the hospital things seem to start ending right there."*

Rating: *2.0*

Excerpt 3:   *"Things are going much better at home. I haven't yelled at the kids or my wife in a couple of weeks. And yet I speak my mind. I feel really pleased about what's happening.*

Rating: *3.0*

Excerpt 4: *"I'm so nervous around new people. Like I'm afraid they'll see I'm having problems. I get disgusted with myself because I know that kind of fear really will limit how much I can help myself."*

Rating: 4.0

Excerpt 5: *"I thought I had it together with my father. It's so discouraging. I can't get myself to say no to him. With all the things I have to do, I'm still driving him to work at four in the morning. If I can't say no, that extra pressure could damn well put me back."*

Rating: 5.0

The rationale for each of the ratings is as follows. The first excerpt is rated 1.0 because the client is basically talking about irrelevancies. All the talk focuses on a detailed description of the car's problems. The second excerpt is rated 2.0 because the client is presenting relevant content. However, the client's reaction to the situation is not talked about. This is in contrast to the third excerpt, rated 3.0, where the client not only tells what happened but also notes his reaction of pleasure. The fourth excerpt receives a 4.0 rating because the client expresses feelings about self (disgust) and talks about why the situation is important to her, that is, the fear limits how much she can help herself. In the fifth response, rated 5.0, the client not only gives a reaction to the situation and why it is important but goes on to introduce the specific personal deficit of not being able to say no.

Practice Situations

In order to further familiarize yourself with the scale, attempt to rate each of the client excerpts below on a scale from 1.0 to 5.0.

Excerpt 1: *"My brother was supposed to pick me up and take me down to the place. Then he didn't show up. It really makes me mad. It seems like he's always acting irresponsibly."*

Rating: _____

Excerpt 2: *Silence. Client does nothing but fidget in her chair.*

Rating: _____

Excerpt 3: *"The nurse came in yesterday and really started buggin' me. I blew my stack and started yelling and carrying on. I really thought I had learned to be able to tell people in authority my feelings in a polite way. But I guess I just can't yet. It's really discouraging."*

Rating: _____

Excerpt 4:   *"Home is really a mess. The house is dirty. The kids are dirty. Meals are just slopped together. Nobody seems to be doing anything."*

Rating: _____

Excerpt 5:   *"I finally found some people I can get along with. We go out and have a good time. I really feel good being with them. It's so great to know there are people whom I feel I can really be myself with."*

Rating: _____

Using the Diagnostic Interviewing Scale, these excerpts would be rated as follows: 3.0, 1.0, 5.0, 2.0, and 4.0. You can figure your rating-accuracy score by taking the *absolute difference* between each of your ratings and the expert ratings, summing these absolute-difference scores, and then dividing the total by 5. Here is an example:

Expert	Your Rating	Absolute Discrepancy
3.0	2.0	1.0
1.0	1.0	0
5.0	5.0	0
2.0	2.5	0.5
4.0	4.0	0
	Sum	1.5
	Score =	$1.5 \div 5 = .3$

If your score is .5 or less, then you can make accurate discriminations about the effectiveness of the client's exploration and understanding. If you reached this level of effectiveness, you can begin assessing where the client is in terms of his or her exploration on each topic. If your discrimination score was greater than .5, however, you will want to restudy the scales and reread the excerpts. You should do this before trying to rate your client's functioning.

Perhaps even more important than assessing the client's level of functioning in the diagnostic interview is assessing the *practitioner's* own level of functioning. As noted in earlier chapters, there is extensive research to indicate that the practitioner's level of skill greatly influences the client's level of exploration and understanding (Carkhuff,

1969). More specifically, this research shows that when the practitioner offers high levels of diagnostic interviewing skills, the client engages in high levels of exploration. When the same practitioner with the same client decreases his or her level of functioning, the client's level of exploration also declines.

The five-point scale that can be used for rating practitioner functioning in the diagnostic interview is presented below:

Practitioner Diagnostic Interviewing Scale

Level 1.0   The practitioner's response *contains no explicit and accurate diagnosis of either the feeling or the content* presented by the client. Either the practitioner makes no attempt to label the feeling and content presented by the client or she or he is inaccurate in the identification made.

Level 2.0   The practitioner's response *contains an explicit and accurate diagnosis of either the feeling or the content* presented by the client *but not both.*

Level 3.0   *The practitioner's response contains an explicit and accurate diagnosis of both the feeling and the content* presented by the client. The practitioner's response is *interchangeable* with the client's expression in that the feeling and content labeled is not more and not less than the feeling and content presented by the client.

Level 4.0   The practitioner's response *contains an explicit and accurate diagnosis of the personal meaning* of the client's expression. That is, the response accurately labels why the experience is significant to the client.

Level 5.0   The practitioner's response *contains an explicit and accurate diagnosis of the client's personal strengths and deficits and his or her feelings about him or herself* because of these characteristics. That is, the response labels the skill behavior that the client has or does not have and the client's feelings about him or herself because of this personal strength or deficit.

As with the client scale, when using the instrument for rating practitioner's behavior, it is possible to rate at the midpoint of each level (i.e., 1.5, 2.5, 3.5, and 4.5). This would be done when the response did not quite make it to the full level. For example, a diagnosis of feeling and content might be off in the intensity of feeling but otherwise be accurate. This would be rated at 2.5 rather than 3.0. As an illustration of the various levels, read the client expression below and the alternative practitioner responses.

Client
Expression: *"I ended up missing work today because I slept right through. I'm so keyed up that I can't get to sleep at night. I haven't really slept in almost a month. Finally, I just stayed up drinking and popping pills and then I really slept. I just can't take this being by myself stuff anymore. I got no family, not any real friends. It's too much. I don't know what to do."*

Response 1: *"How long has this been going on?"*

Response 2: *"It sounds like this incident has you really scared."*

Response 3: *"Having no one is really frightening to you."*

Response 4: *"You're terrified that you just may end up destroying yourself."*

Response 5: *"You feel scared because you can't identify the changes you need to make in order to reach out to others to get the relationships you crave."*

These responses would be rated 1.0, 2.0, 3.0, 4.0, and 5.0. Response number 1 simply asks a question and labels neither content nor feeling. Response number 2 captures the feeling but does not attend to the content in any way. Response number 3 diagnoses the feeling and content presented by the client. The fourth response gets at the personal meaning of the situation — that it could lead to death. The fifth response has a deficit behavior; thus, it is rated 5.0.

Practice Situations

Now practice your rating skills. Read the client statement below and the alternative practitioner responses. Then rate each one from 1.0 to 5.0.

Client
Statement: *"It's not an easy thing to talk about. I guess the heart of the problem is sort of a sexual problem. I just don't get the fulfillment out of it as I used to. I don't think it's enjoyable for my husband either, although we don't discuss it. I find myself being sexually attracted to other men. I don't... I just don't know.*

Response 1: *"You feel really worried because something is wrong with your sexual life, although you're not sure why."*

Response 2: *"It makes you pretty damn anxious because for some reason you don't understand why you are losing something with someone who is so important to you."*

Response 3: *"You feel discouraged because you can't respond sexually or even talk to your husband about something this important."*

Response 4: *"What about your other relationships with your husband and his role as father and companion?"*

Response 5: *"You're saying that your marriage is deteriorating physically and you don't know what this means."*

These responses should be rated as follows: 3.0, 4.0, 5.0, 1.0, and 2.0. Again, you may calculate your discrimination score by taking the absolute difference between your ratings and the expert ratings, adding the difference scores, and dividing by 5. If you achieve a discrimination score of .5 or less, you are ready to begin to evaluate your own or others' diagnostic interviewing skills. If your average discrepancy was greater than .5, you should reread this material before attempting to make real-life discriminations.

In making real-life discriminations, you can make ratings of an interview up to level 3.0 simply by listening to two- or three-minute segments and rating the modal level of functioning. Responses at 4.0 and 5.0 require a base of continuous level 3.0 responding and may not be appropriate in this brief a segment. Thus, to rate above 3.0, it will be necessary to listen to the discussion of the whole topic and rate the highest level of diagnostic response that was made by the practitioner *and* accepted by the client. If you are rating your own interviews, you may be able to simply recall the highest-level diagnostic statement made and the client's response.

You should practice rating your own sessions both on tape and by recall. Remember, it is not enough to make a diagnostically accurate statement. The client's reaction to your statement should indicate that she or he accepted your comments.

By using the Practitioner and Client Diagnostic Interviewing Process Scales, the practitioner is able to judge the effectiveness of the diagnostic interview at any given moment in time for any particular subject area. Besides using tapes to rate interviews after the fact, the practitioner who has a working knowledge of these scales can use them to rate the client's and his or her responses as they occur within the interview. Thus, the practitioner has immediate feedback as to the level of the client's and his or her verbalizations and whether or not the level is increasing as more time is spent on each subject area. Thus, the practitioner can make an ongoing diagnosis of the interview *process* itself while it is actually occurring.

As indicated before, the product of the diagnostic planning process is the assessment of the client's and significant other's relevant strengths and deficits as recorded on the Client Assessment Chart and the Environmental Assessment Chart. These charts constitute another means for evaluating the effectiveness of the diagnostic planning process. The following five-point Assessment Chart Scale can be used to provide a rating of how well or poorly each skill behavior has been assessed.

Assessment Chart Scale

For each critical skill behavior that has been identified, score 1 point for each assessment step correctly taken. If none of these assessment steps have been completed, the practitioner receives an overall score of 1 for that particular skill strength or deficit. Each assessment step correctly taken adds 1 point to the score. Thus the scale scores can range from level 1 to level 5.

Score	Skill
1 point:	Skill behavior is *categorized* with respect to its relevant environmental area, that is, *where* it needs to be performed.
1 point:	Skill behavior assessment indicates *"who"* performs the behavior.
1 point:	Skill behavior is *operationalized* in a way that allows the behavior to be *measured and observed*.
1 point:	Skill behavior is *quantified* in terms of the person's *present* and needed *levels* of functioning.

The Client and Environmental Assessment Charts that have been used as examples in this text contain skill behaviors that have been assessed at level 5 on this scale. The practitioner's assessment goal is to obtain ratings of 5 for each relevant skill behavior. The extent to which this has been accomplished is an indication of diagnostic planning outcome.

A method of using the Diagnostic Planning Charts for evaluation is to examine the Diagnostic Planning Chart (use Table 21 for an example) and to compute the percentage of skill characteristics that the client has initialed. Remember, the client's initialing was an observable indication that he or she understood and agreed with the importance of this skill. Thus, the percentage of behaviors that have been initialed will give a rough index of how successful the practitioner has been in gaining the *client's* acceptance of the diagnostic plan.

A final method of evaluating the effectiveness of diagnostic planning may be to obtain some measure of various people's satisfaction with the rehabilitation diagnostic process. These people might include the client, significant others, the referral source who instigated the rehabilitation referral, and other treatment personnel. These individuals can be asked to fill out a very brief form such as the following:

Diagnostic Planning Satisfaction Scale

Read these statements: *Circle your answers:*

1) I understand exactly the particular *behaviors* that are important in the client's rehabilitation plan.   Yes   No

2) I understand *in what environments* these behaviors are important.   Yes   No

3) I understand *who* must perform each behavior.   Yes   No

4) I understand the person's *present level* of functioning on these important behaviors.   Yes   No

5) I understand the person's *needed level* of functioning on these important behaviors.   Yes   No

6) In general, I am satisfied with the diagnostic planning process.   Yes   No

The use of this form or variations of it will provide the practitioner with important feedback as to how the practitioner's diagnostic planning efforts are being perceived.

The methods of evaluating diagnostic planning effectiveness are numerous because the process and outcome of diagnostic planning are observable and, thus, are capable of being measured and evaluated.

Because of this, the practitioner should be able to constantly improve his or her diagnostic planning skills; the feedback is there for the asking.

173

SUMMARY

This section on evaluating diagnostic planning skills brings this text to its completion. You have explored, come to understand, and acted to learn a very complex process. In particular, you are now capable of more effectively helping a client to *explore* in detail his or her unique rehabilitation situation through the use of your informing, encouraging, attending, observing, listening, responding, and problem and goal specification skills. You are now better equipped to *understand* and help your clients understand their personal strengths and deficits. This has been accomplished through your acquisition of skills in personalizing and categorizing client strengths and deficits. Finally, you are better prepared to *assess* your client's personal strengths and deficits because of your increased skill in operationalizing behavior and identifying present and needed levels of functioning.

This text has taught the various diagnostic planning skills in discrete steps. This step-by-step process is the most efficient way to learn skills. Once these skills are mastered, however, the diagnostic practitioner will be capable of modifying and adapting his or her diagnostic skills based on the client's unique situation. The diagnostic system is not used for the purpose of controlling the practitioner and client interaction — but rather for guiding it. It serves to keep both the practitioner and client on track and working together toward the diagnostic goal. It is a system that uses familiar and understandable terms. So often the psychiatrically disabled client is devalued because the treatment system uses techniques that seem mysterious. The general public (and often the client) may reject the mental health system because they are not able to comprehend or relate to the vocabulary and methods used by the treatment system.

In contrast, because rehabilitation outcome is to a great extent a function of the client's involvement in his or her own rehabilitation, the rehabilitation diagnostic system must try to maximize that involvement. Although this serves to make the rehabilitation intervention less mysterious, it does not make it easy.

There is no doubt that comprehensive rehabilitation diagnostic planning is hard work. But if the function of the rehabilitation practitioner is to rehabilitate, then attaining that goal should be worth whatever price is needed — even hard work!

REFERENCES

Anthony, W. A. *Principles of psychiatric rehabilitation.* Amherst, Mass: Human Resource Development Press, 1979.

Anthony, W. A., Buell, G. J., Sharratt, S., & Althoff, M. E. The efficacy of psychiatric rehabilitation. *Psychological Bulletin,* 1972, *78,* 447-456.

Anthony, W. A., & Carkhuff, R. R. Effects of rehabilitation counselor training upon trainee functioning. *Rehabilitation Counseling Bulletin,* 1970, *13,* 333-342.

Anthony, W. A., & Carkhuff, R. R. The functional professional therapeutic agent. In A. Gurman & A. Razin (Eds.), *Effective psychotherapy.* Oxford, England: Pergamon Press, 1977, pp. 103-119.

Anthony, W. A., Cohen, M. R., & Vitalo, R. The measurement of rehabilitation outcome. *Schizophrenia Bulletin,* 1978, *4,* 365-383.

Anthony, W. A., & Margules, A. Toward improving the efficacy of psychiatric rehabilitation: A skills training approach. *Rehabilitation Psychology,* 1974, *21,* 101-105.

Aspy, D., & Roebuck, F. *KIDS.* Amherst, Mass: Human Resource Development Press, 1978.

Barker, L. L. *Listening Behavior.* Englewood Cliffs, N.J.: Prentice-Hall, 1971.

Berenson, B. G., & Mitchell, K. M. *Confrontation: For better or for worse.* Amherst, Mass: Human Resource Development Press, 1974.

Bolton, B. Client and counselor perspectives in the assessment of client adjustment. *Rehabilitation Counseling Bulletin,* June 1978, 282-291.

Cannon, J. R., & Pierce, R. M. Order effects in the experimental manipulation of therapeutic conditions. *Journal of Clinical Psychology,* 1968, *24,* 242-244.

Carkhuff, R. R. *Helping and human relations: Volumes 1 & 2,* New York: Holt, Rinehart & Winston, 1969.

Carkhuff, R. R., Kratochvil, D., & Friel, T. The effects of professional training: The communication and discrimination of the facilitative conditions. *Journal of Counseling Psychology,* 1968, *15,* 68-74.

Eysenck, H. J. The effects of psychotherapy: An evaluation. *Journal of Consulting Psychology,* 1952, *16,* 319-324.

Eysenck, H. J. The effect of psychotherapy. In H. J. Eysenck (Ed.), *Handbook of abnormal psychology.* London: Pitman, 1960.

Eysenck, H. J. New approaches to mental illness: The failure of a tradition. In H. Gottesfeld (Ed.), *The critical issues of community mental health.* New York: Behavioral Publications, 1972.

Garfield, S. L. Research on client variables in psychotherapy. In A. E. Bergin & S. L. Garfield (Eds.), *Handbook of psychotherapy and behavior change: An empirical analysis.* New York: Wiley & Sons, 1971.

Genther, R. W., & Moughan, J. Introverts and extroverts responses to nonverbal attending behavior. *Journal of Counseling Psychology,* 1977, *24,* 144-146.

Holder, B. T., Carkhuff, R. R., & Berenson, B. G. The differential effects of the manipulation of therapeutic conditions upon high and low functioning clients. *Journal of Counseling Psychology,* 1967, *14,* 63-66.

Mehrabian, A. *Nonverbal Communication.* New York: Alding-Atherton, 1972.

Mickelson, D. J., & Stevic, R. R. Differential effects of facilitative and nonfacilitative behavioral counselors. *Journal of Counseling Psychology,* 1971, *18,* 314-317.

Piaget, G., Berenson, B. G., & Carkhuff, R. R. The differential effects of the manipulation of therapeutic conditions by high and low functioning counselors upon high and low functioning clients. *Journal of Consulting Psychology,* 1967, *31,* 481-486.

Schless, A. P., & Mendels, J. The value of interviewing family and friends in assessing life stressors. *Archives of General Psychiatry,* 1978, *35,* 565-567.

Smith, D. L. Goal attainment scaling as an adjunct to counseling. *Journal of Counseling Psychology,* 1976, *23,* 22-27.

Smith-Hanen, S. S. Effects of nonverbal behaviors on judged levels of counselor warmth and empathy. *Journal of Counseling Psychology,* 1977, *24,* 87-91.

Sue, S., McKinney, H., Allen, D. B. Predictors of the duration of therapy for clients in the community mental health center system. *Community Mental Health Journal,* 1976, *12,* 365-375

Sue, S., McKinney, H., Allen, D., & Hall, I. Delivery of community mental health services to black and white clients. *Journal of Consulting and Clinical Psychology,* 1974, *43,* 794-801.

Truax, C. B., & Carkhuff, R. R. The experimental manipulation of therapeutic conditions. *Journal of Consulting Psychology,* 1965, *29,* 119-124.

Truax, C. B., & Carkhuff, R. R. Toward effective counseling and psychotherapy. Chicago: Aldine, 1967.

Vitalo, R. The effects of facilitative interpersonal functioning in a conditioning paradigm. *Journal of Counseling Psychology,* 1970, *17,* 141-144.

Vitalo, R., & Farcas, M. Physical fitness as a component in psychiatric rehabilitation. In W. Anthony, *The principles of psychiatric rehabilitation.* Amherst, Mass: Human Resource Development Press, 1979.

Walker, R. A. The ninth panacea: Program evaluation. *Evaluation,* 1972, *1,* 45-53.

Walls, R. T., & Masson, C. Rehabilitation client problems and family communications. *Rehabilitation Counseling Bulletin,* June 1978, 317-324.

Wolkon, G. W. Characteristics of clients and continuity of care into the community. *Community Mental Health Journal,* 1970, *6,* 215-221.